The Parent's Handbook

STEP

Systematic Training for Effective Parenting

Don Dinkmeyer, Ph.D.
Gary D. McKay, Ph.D.

AGS ®

American Guidance Service
Circle Pines, Minn. 55014

To the encouragers, our wives and sons:

E. Jane and Joyce
Don, Jim, and Rob

To our teacher, friend,
and source of encouragement:

Rudolf Dreikurs

Distributed to the regular book trade by Random House, Inc.

Cover design: Terry Dugan
Illustrations: John Robb
Cover photograph: Steve Niedorf

Library of Congress Card Number: 81-20481
ISBN 0-913476-80-3
ISBN 0-394-71031-2 (Random House)

Contents

Introduction

We believe that being an effective parent is one of the most rewarding tasks in life — and it's also one of the most challenging. Part of the challenge involves sorting out all of the conflicting theories of child training one finds in books, newspapers, and on television. It's so easy to become confused!

STEP (Systematic Training for Effective Parenting) provides a practical approach to parent-child relations. *The Parent's Handbook* is your guide to a democratic philosophy of child training that we and more than *one million parents* have found to be effective. STEP will work for you and your family, if you put into practice the techniques and principles presented in *The Parent's Handbook*. Success will depend on your commitment and involvement.

We suggest that you pace yourself by spending a week on each chapter — nine weeks in all. Read a chapter at the beginning of the week; then during the week, study the problem situation, the questions, and the charts that follow the chapter. Be sure to take time to carry out the activity for the week.

Many parents choose to enhance their STEP experience by joining a STEP support group. Tens of thousands of groups have been set up to give parents the opportunity to discuss ideas and share experiences. Turn to page 119 for more information about parent groups and the complete STEP program.

Through diligent study and application — whether on your own or in a group — you will "graduate" as a more effective parent. If you're willing to stick with it, we're confident that STEP will help you reap the rewards of parenting.

Don Dinkmeyer, Ph.D.
Diplomate of Counseling Psychology
American Board of Professional Psychology
President, Communication and Motivation
    Training Institute, Inc. (CMTI)
Coral Springs, Florida

Gary D. McKay, Ph.D.
Educational and Psychological Consultant
Clinical Member, American Association for
    Marriage and Family Therapy
President, Communication and Motivation
    Training Institute-West, Inc. (CMTI-West)
Tucson, Arizona

CHAPTER 1

Understanding Children's Behavior and Misbehavior

Consider the following scene.

Mrs. A: It's good that you could come over, Jean. We haven't had a chance to talk for a long time.

Mrs. B: I know, Sue. It seems that things just keep piling up.

Girl: Mom, can I go to Barbara's house?

Mrs. A: No, Kay, you know you've been sick. The doctor told you to stay in bed and rest.

Girl: Aww, Mom, I feel better, and I'm getting bored. Can't I go over for just a little while?

Mrs. A: No. Now get back in bed!

Girl: (crying) I don't want to go to bed. I'm OK. I want to go to Barbara's!

Mrs. A: (angry) Kay! You heard me! Get to bed this instant!

Girl: (stomps off, crying) You never let me do anything!

Mrs. A: (embarrassed) I'm sorry, Jean.

Mrs. B: (laughs) No need to apologize. The same thing happens at my house.

Mrs. A: Children are so different today. When I was a child, I never questioned my mother.

Mrs. B: Neither did I. I don't understand why, but there seems to be no respect for authority these days.

These mothers are like many other parents today. They recognize that their children's attitudes often seem different from the attitudes the parents held when they were children. Parents are often confused about this.

STEP is designed to help parents relate more effectively to their children. It provides training for people who want to become more effective parents.

Why do parents need training?

For a long time, our society has demanded special training for all kinds of workers who deal with children — for teachers, counselors, psychologists, social workers, child psychiatrists. But the persons who are important in children's lives—the parents—have been taking up the task of child-rearing usually without special training.

Today the need for training parents is becoming well recognized for a number of reasons, all related to social change. Our society's general shift from an autocratic attitude to a democratic attitude and toward social equality has presented challenges which most people, especially parents, are not well prepared to meet.

In the more rigid, autocratic society in which most of today's parents were reared, relationships between people were understood in terms of a pecking order: of superiors and inferiors. In the home, Father was considered the supreme authority. Mother was supposed to be subservient to him, and the children were supposed to be subservient to both of them. Society was well ordered: people "knew their places." If our society had retained its rigid structure, many of our present social problems would not have developed. But society is not static, and vast changes have culminated in fundamental questions about the proper basis for social order.

Certain groups formerly considered to be inferior grew tired of their positions. Unions were formed to protect workers' rights. Minorities demanded equal treatment with those in the favored positions. Women challenged the principle of male supremacy.

These challenges to basic assumptions have produced a society radically different from the autocratic society of the past. We are becoming a social system in which all people insist upon being treated as equals.

Of course, children have been influenced by this change in social relationships. Perhaps the most significant influence on relationships between adults and children has been the change in relationships between men and women. The women's liberation movement, widely publicized in recent years, has been developing for some time. Before World War I, women were demanding acknowledgement of their right to vote. During World War II, women entered the work force in vast numbers. After the war, many women remained on the job for personal satisfaction and to provide additional income for family luxuries. Increased numbers of women also went to college and entered professions.

With increasing awareness of their rights and abilities, women became more insistent that their legal and economic status be improved. Many men have reacted defensively to the women's liberation movement.

Thus, competition between individual men and women develops within the framework of a social revolution. Children born into a family in which there is a struggle for supremacy or for individual rights easily conclude that they have rights, too. However, children do not as easily understand that the democratic way to establish one's own

rights is to respect the rights of others. Children today tend to believe that they should have the rights and parents should have the responsibility. By overprotecting our children from the consequences of irresponsibility, we have fostered this lopsided understanding of rights and responsibilities.

But the matter does not stop there. In seeking their rights, today's children are not willing to submit to the arbitrary rule of adults. Thus, the traditional technique for winning obedience from children — dispensing rewards and punishments — is no longer as effective as it once was. Only when children recognize adults as superior do they believe adults have the right to punish them.

Today's children tend to consider rewards to be their right. Parents who rely on rewards often find that a child performs only when rewarded and will not respond to rewards unless the payment seems to be worth the effort. A candy bar for a five-year-old may become an automobile in adolescence.

Neither is punishment as effective as it once was. Children have reasoned, "If you have the right to punish me, I have the right to punish you." If punishment works at all, it is effective only when it's constantly repeated.

Our dilemma, then, is: What shall we do? How shall we meet the challenges of raising today's children? If we could return to the more autocratic society of the past, our problems with children might diminish. But this would require return to a superior-inferior pattern of relationships inconsistent with the principles of democracy. Furthermore, those who have gained their rights are not willing to give them up. An alternative might be a turn toward permissiveness — placing fewer restrictions on children's behavior. But permissiveness would produce more chaos than we presently have. No society can survive without placing some limits on the behavior of its members.

Social Equality of Parents and Children

In a democracy, each person must behave responsibly. If we are to develop responsible adults, we must begin in the home by developing responsible children. Because reward and punishment are not as effective as they were in the past, we need to create new relationships between children and adults. Since social equality is the ideal toward which the "democratic revolution" is striving, these new child-rearing procedures must be based on democratic principles.

Democratic child-training procedures are based on principles of equality and mutual respect. We must be careful not to define equality in terms of sameness. Obviously, adults and children are not the same. In addition to physical differences, adults are usually more knowledgeable and experienced and have certain legal and economic rights, privileges, and responsibilities that children do not have. Therefore, by "equality" we mean that children are equal to adults in terms of *human worth* and *dignity*. In a democracy, every person is entitled to respect and to self-determination within limits prescribed by the society.

Democracy permits choice. The democratic parent provides opportunities for children to make decisions, within limits, and to be accountable for these decisions. Through STEP you will become familiar with a disciplinary technique that replaces reward and punishment, permits choice, and allows children to be responsible for their own decisions. It develops *self-discipline.* This alternative to reward and punishment is called "natural and logical consequences."

The democratic parent also uses encouragement. This implies valuing the child as a unique individual who requires love and respect. In a later session, you will learn specific techniques for encouraging your children.

In this age of influence and persuasion, contrasted with yesteryear's control and domination, it is essential that parents learn to understand their child's behavior, misbehavior, and emotions. We will devote the remainder of this chapter and part of Chapter 2, to understanding the child.

Understanding Behavior

There are several popular ways to explain children's behavior. Some people believe behavior is primarily the result of heredity. Others believe behavior depends mainly on environmental influences — on the people and events surrounding the child. There is also a common belief that children go through stages which occur predictably around certain ages. Let's examine each of these ideas briefly.

Although it's generally recognized that children are born with certain traits of temperament, the fact of direct inheritance of personality traits has never been established. If behavior is primarily the result of heredity, why do children of the same family have widely differing personalities?

The theory that behavior is caused by one's environment raises another interesting question: If behavior is environmentally caused, why do individuals react with wide variations to the same circumstances? Those who believe that behavior is caused, by either internal or external forces, do not admit the creative capacity of individuals to make decisions — to choose how they will respond to physical or environmental conditions.

Parents also hear a lot about ages and stages. "The terrible two's!" "All five-year-olds do that!" "Don't worry; he's just going through a stage." "All girls her age . . ." "He'll grow out of it." and so on. Although children do appear to have "stages" of oppositional reaction to adults, this should not be used as a reason for accepting inappropriate behavior.

Experience shows there are many exceptions to these so-called rules and that uncooperative children do not always "grow out of" that attitude. Instead they are probably in the process of establishing a pattern of behavior.

Sex-role stereotypes, such as "Boys will be boys" and "Girls are naturally more manageable," have influenced us to *anticipate* and *reinforce* certain behaviors. Typically we have expected — and there is considerable power in expectation — that girls would be cooperative and that boys would rebel or be lazy. Girls have been rewarded for being mothers' helpers, and boys have not been expected to be helpful. Thus, sex-role stereotypes have come to be seen as "natural."

In addition, we have come to accept annoying, uncooperative, and rebellious behavior in children as "normal." We expect and accept negative behavior in the belief that we can do nothing about it.

The problem lies in our lack of understanding of human behavior and in our belief that we are powerless to influence our children to behave more cooperatively. We need to realize that our children's misbehavior is not the result of an age or a stage. It may be typical; but we need not expect it, accept it, or consider it normal. Parents who understand children's behavior and misbehavior are in a much better position to influence their children.

The STEP approach begins with the recognition that all behavior occurs for a social *purpose*. People are decision-making social beings whose main goal in life is to *belong*. Each of us strives continually to find and maintain a place of significance. In our search we select beliefs, feelings, and behavior which we feel will gain us significance. Behavior can best be understood by observing its consequences.

In Chapter 2, we will discuss our emotional growth. For now, let's continue our efforts to understand why our children misbehave. Our study will show there are purposes behind misbehavior. Understanding these purposes will make us more effective parents.

Four Goals of Misbehavior

Misbehaving children are discouraged. They do not believe they can belong in useful ways. Therefore, they seek to belong through misbehavior.

Rudolf Dreikurs, a prominent psychiatrist, classified children's misbehavior into four broad categories. Dreikurs called these categories "goals" in the sense that the misbehavior achieved something for a child. These goals remain present in the behavior of older children and adults, but additional purposes influence misbehavior as we mature.

Although the four goals seem complex at first, we have found that any parent can learn how to discover the purpose of a child's misbehavior by using two simple techniques. Remember that since misbehavior serves a purpose, it is best understood by observing its *consequences,* thus:

1. Observe your own reaction to the child's misbehavior. YOUR FEELINGS point to the child's goals.

2. Observe the child's response to your attempts at correction. THE CHILD'S RESPONSE TO YOUR BEHAVIOR will also let you know what the child is after.

In sum: *train yourself to look at the results of misbehavior rather than just at the misbehavior.* The results of the misbehavior reveal its purpose.

With these techniques in mind, let's consider Dreikurs' four goals of misbehavior.

Attention

The first goal Dreikurs identified is the goal of attention. The desire for attention is almost universal in young children.

Children prefer to gain attention in useful ways; but if they can't get it that way, they seek attention in useless ways. Children who hold the conviction that they can belong only if they are receiving attention prefer negative attention to being ignored.

Following our two-step guideline, we would check the consequences of the child's misbehavior to see whether the goal was attention. If we are merely *annoyed* and correct the child's misbehavior by *reminding* or *coaxing,* the child has received the desired attention. Also, if the child's response has been to *stop the misbehavior temporarily,* the goal of attention has been reached. Later, the child will probably repeat the act or do something else to seek attention.

To help attention-seeking children, we must change our responses to show them that they can achieve significance through useful contributions rather than through useless bids for attention or service. We must focus on their con-

structive behavior; we must either ignore the misbehavior or pay attention to it in ways they don't expect.

Attention should not be given on demand, even for positive acts, because this reinforces inappropriate desire for attention. Children easily come to believe that if they are not "center stage," they do not belong.

The appropriate way to give attention is to give it when it is not expected. This places emphasis upon giving rather than getting. We realize that at this point, these sound like oversimplified, quick solutions. But for now we are interested only in your understanding the general idea of how to stop reinforcing misbehavior.

Further on you will learn more specific ways to deal with the four goals of misbehavior.

Power

Power-seeking children feel they are significant only when they are boss. They seek to do only what they want. "No one can force me to do anything" or "You better do what I want." Even if parents do succeed in subduing them, the victory is only temporary. Parents may win the argument, but lose the relationship.

When a child is defiant, parents feel *angry* and *provoked.* Attempts to correct the child are seldom successful. The child will *defy* the parents and *continue the unacceptable behavior, or* will *stop temporarily* and *then continue with more intensity.* Some children in power struggles do what they are told, but not in a way the parents want it done. We call this "defiant compliance."

As a rule, when dealing with power-seeking children, adults must refrain from getting angry and must disengage themselves from the power struggle. Using power tactics to counter children's bids for power only impresses them with the value of power and increases their desire for it.

If the struggle for power continues and the children come to feel they cannot defeat the parents, they may alter the desire for power and pursue the third goal, revenge.

Revenge

Children who pursue revenge are convinced that they are not lovable; that they are significant only when they are able to hurt others as they believe they have been hurt. They find a place by being cruel and disliked.

Parents of the revengeful child feel *deeply hurt* and *want to retaliate.* The child responds to their counterattack by *seeking further revenge,* either by intensifying the misbehavior or by choosing another sort of weapon. These parents need to realize that the child's revengeful behavior stems from discouragement and is not necessarily "caused" by the parents.

To begin to help the revengeful child, parents must be on guard not to retaliate. As difficult as it will be, they must improve their relationship

with the child by remaining calm and showing good will.

If the war of revenge continues between parents and children, and the children come to feel utterly defeated, they may give up and seek to be excused for their behavior by displaying inadequacy.

Display of Inadequacy

Children who display inadequacy, or disability, are *extremely* discouraged. Since they have given up hope of succeeding, they attempt to keep others from expecting anything of them, either. Giving up may be total or only in areas where children feel they can't succeed.

Parents will know that a child is pursuing this goal if they, too, *feel despair* and *want to give up* — if they feel like "throwing up their hands." The child *responds passively or fails to respond* to whatever the parents do. *The child does not improve.*

To help a child who feels inadequate, parents must eliminate all criticism, and focus, instead, on the child's assets and strengths. The parents must encourage any effort to improve, no matter how small it seems.

Although we presented the four goals of misbehavior in a progression from attention-getting through power, revenge, and display of inadequacy, *children may not follow this course,* because they select their goals according to their perceptions. For example: a pampered child who passively seeks attention may progress directly to displaying inadequacy if he or she sees the parents' overprotection as proof of their lack of confidence in the child. Like children who have been abused, pampered children may conclude that they are powerless to overcome the difficulties of life.

Remember that *all misbehavior* — even the inappropriate bid for attention — *stems from discouragement.* The child lacks courage to behave in an active, constructive manner. A child does not misbehave unless he or she feels a real or threatened loss of status. Whatever goal the misbehavior serves, it is done in the belief that only in this way can the child have a place in the

group. On occasion, a child may change goals, depending on how she or he interprets a situation. Or, a child may use the same misbehavior for different goals, or behave in different ways for the same purpose. We can discover the goal a child seeks only by observing the results. Once we discover the goal, we are in a position to begin redirecting the child.

Although they are often aware of the consequences of their misbehavior, *children are usually unaware of their goals.*

By now, it should be clear that children's behavior and intentions toward us will change only if we change our approaches. *Although we do not cause children to misbehave, we can reinforce and encourage their misbehavior and their selection of faulty goals by reacting in ways they expect.* Therefore, we must concentrate on changing our own behavior if we wish children to change theirs.

Children may pursue the goals of misbehavior either actively or passively, with the exception of the fourth goal. (Since goal four, display of inadequacy, involves giving up, a child pursuing this goal can behave only passively.) Chart 1A, on page 14, describes the four goals, or purposes, of misbehavior.

The Four Basic Ingredients for Building Positive Relationships

No child-training techniques will be effective unless you are willing to take the time and make the effort to build a positive relationship with your children. The following four ingredients are essential for effective parent-child relationships.

Mutual Respect

Problems between human beings of any age are usually the result of a lack of mutual respect. Parents often complain that their children do not respect them. They seem not to realize that respect is earned; that it comes from showing respect to others. Nagging, yelling, hitting, talking down, doing things for children that they can do for themselves, following double standards — all show lack of respect. (Ask yourself: Do you require your children to knock before entering your bedroom, but feel free to barge into theirs?)

To establish mutual respect, we must be willing to begin by demonstrating respect for our children. A good way to start is to minimize your negative talk. Talk with your children when the atmosphere is friendly.

In STEP you will learn many other ways to deal with children on a basis of mutual respect.

Taking Time for Fun

In the busy pace of modern life, it's often easy to overlook this important aspect for building a positive family relationship. Actually, however, it doesn't take as much time as we think. The important ingredient of time together is *quality*, not *quantity*. An hour of positive relationship is worth more than several hours of conflict.

We suggest that you take time for fun. Spend some time each day with each of your children, doing what you *both* enjoy. The fun is spoiled if one person or the other feels forced to do something. In two-parent families, the father and mother often divide the time spent alone with each child each day, and then alternate days. Bedtime is favored by many as a pleasant time together. The important thing is that you and your children jointly plan the way you will spend your time. Each child will know that he or she will have his or her special time with you. If another child interferes, all you have to say is, "This is (John's) and my time together. You and I will be together at the time we agreed upon."

In addition to individual times, the family needs to spend time having fun as a family at least once a week.

Encouragement

We must believe in our children if they are to believe in themselves. To feel adequate, children need frequent encouragement. A cooperative relationship depends on how children feel about themselves and how they feel about you.

Chart 1B, on page 15, gives positive counterparts to the four goals of misbehavior and suggests how to encourage the positive. Chapter 3 deals specifically with encouragement. Here it is sufficient to point out that encouragement essentially involves minimizing the importance of children's mistakes while recognizing their assets and strengths.

Communicating Love

How often do you tell your children, by words and actions, that you love them? To feel secure each child must have at least one significant person to love and to be loved by. Telling your children that you love them, especially when they are not anticipating such a comment, and nonverbal signs such as pats, hugs, kisses, and tousling hair are extremely important.

You need to realize that love is also communicated by the way you relate to your children in general—through your attitude of mutual respect, and through your allowing them to develop responsibility and independence.

QUESTIONS

1. The reading states that today's parents need training. What has happened in society to make this training necessary?

2. Why is reward and punishment as a method of discipline no longer as effective as it was in the past?

3. The authors suggest using democratic procedures with children as an alternative to the autocratic methods of reward and punishment. What do they mean by "democratic procedures"?

4. What do the authors believe about human behavior? How does this apply to children?

5. Why do children misbehave? What are the four goals of misbehavior?

6. What are two techniques you can use to discover the goal of your child's misbehavior? How do you know if your child is seeking the goal of attention? Power? Revenge? Display of inadequacy? Why is it important to know what goal the child is seeking?

7. In general, what do the authors say we should do when our children inappropriately seek attention? When they seek power? When they seek revenge? When they display inadequacy?

8. Why do we need to concentrate on changing our own behavior rather than concentrate on changing the child's behavior?

9. What are the four basic ingredients for building a positive relationship?

PROBLEM SITUATION

Five-year-old Jamie is very shy. When he goes out with Mother and they meet one of her friends, Jamie hides behind his mother and sucks his thumb. Mother tries to coax him to come out and say hello to her friend, but Jamie just hides his head and continues to suck his thumb. Mother sighs and apologizes to her friend: "Jamie is so shy. I guess it's a stage he's going through."

1. What is the purpose of Jamie's behavior?
2. How did you make your decision about the purpose?

3. How can shyness be an expression of a desire for power?
4. Describe how a child might use shyness to serve purposes other than power.

ACTIVITY FOR THE WEEK

During the coming week, analyze your children's misbehavior according to one of the four goals described in this chapter: Attention, Power, Revenge, and Display of Inadequacy. Use the following steps:

1. Describe what your child did.
2. Describe your feelings and exactly how you reacted.
3. Describe how the child responded to your reaction.
4. Considering your feelings and the child's response to your corrective efforts, decide what must have been the purpose of the child's behavior.

Also, look for evidence of positive goals and encourage them.

The Goals of Misbehavior

Child's Faulty Belief	Child's Goal*	Parent's Feeling and Reaction	Child's Response to Parent's Attempts at Correction	Alternatives for Parents
I belong *only* when I am being noticed or served.	Attention	FEELING: Annoyed. REACTION: Tendency to remind and coax.	Temporarily stops misbehavior. Later resumes same behavior or disturbs in another way.	Ignore misbehavior when possible. Give attention for positive behavior when child is not making a bid for it. Avoid undue service. Realize that reminding, punishing, rewarding, coaxing, and service are undue attention.
I belong *only* when I am in control or am boss, or when I am proving no one can boss me!	Power	FEELING: Angry; provoked; as if one's authority is threatened. REACTION: Tendency to fight or to give in.	Active- or passive-aggressive misbehavior is intensified, or child submits with "defiant compliance."	Withdraw from conflict. Help child see how to use power constructively by appealing for child's help and enlisting cooperation. Realize that fighting or giving in only increases child's desire for power.
I belong *only* by hurting others as I feel hurt. I cannot be loved.	Revenge	FEELING: Deeply hurt. REACTION: Tendency to retaliate and get even.	Seeks further revenge by intensifying misbehavior or choosing another weapon.	Avoid feeling hurt. Avoid punishment and retaliation. Build trusting relationship; convince child that she or he is loved.
I belong *only* by convincing others not to expect anything from me. I am unable; I am helpless.	Display of Inadequacy	FEELING: Despair; hopelessness. "I give up." REACTION: Tendency to agree with child that nothing can be done.	Passively responds or fails to respond to whatever is done. Shows no improvement.	Stop all criticism. Encourage any positive attempt, no matter how small; focus on assets. Above all, don't be hooked into pity, and don't give up.

*To determine your child's goal, you must check your feelings *and* the child's response to your attempts to correct him or her. Goal identification is simplified by observing:

    a. Your own feelings and reaction to the child's misbehavior.

    b. The child's response to your attempts at correction.

By considering your situation in terms of the chart, you will be able to identify the goal of the misbehavior.

The Goals of Positive Behavior

Child's Belief	Goal	Behavior	How to Encourage Positive Goals
I belong by contributing.	**Attention** **Involvement** **Contribution**	Helps. Volunteers.	Let child know the contribution counts and that you appreciate it.
I can decide and be responsible for my behavior.	**Power** **Autonomy** **Responsibility for own behavior**	Shows self-discipline. Does own work. Is resourceful.	Encourage child's decision making. Let child experience both positive and negative outcomes. Express confidence in child.
I am interested in cooperating.	**Justice** **Fairness**	Returns kindness for hurt. Ignores belittling comments.	Let child know you appreciate her or his interest in cooperating.
I can decide to withdraw from conflict.	**Withdrawal from conflict** **Refusal to fight** **Acceptance of others' opinions**	Ignores provocations. Withdraws from power contest to decide own behavior.	Recognize child's effort to act maturely.

Understanding Behavior

1. Effective parenting requires patience. Take one STEP at a time.

2. Becoming liberated through democratic relationships makes all members of the family more responsible and more capable.

3. Democratic procedures are based on equality and mutual respect.

4. Democratic procedures permit choice.

5. All behavior has a social purpose. The goals of misbehavior are: attention, power, revenge, or display of inadequacy.

6. Your reactions and feelings about a child's misbehavior point to the purpose of that behavior.

7. The child's behavior can most effectively be influenced by changing your own behavior. Responsible children are influenced by responsible parents.

8. When the child is misbehaving, do what she or he does not expect, that is, consider doing exactly the opposite from what you would typically do.

9. Show appreciation for the child's positive behaviors, unless they are meant only to gain attention.

10. Withdraw from power struggles.

11. Because retaliation stimulates further revenge, do not retaliate with the revengeful child. Express good will to improve the quality of the relationship.

12. Focus on the child's assets and strengths, rather than on finding fault.

13. Showing confidence in the child will help the child develop self-confidence.

14. A child who seeks power often has a parent who likes to boss others.

15. A child who displays inadequacy is not unable; rather, the child lacks belief in his or her ability.

My Plan for Improving Relationships

(An opportunity to assess progress each week)

My specific concern:

My usual response:

☐ talking, lecturing   ☐ punishing, removing privileges, shaming

☐ noticing, nagging   ☐ threatening, warning

☐ becoming angry   ☐ other_____

My progress this week:

	I am doing this more	I am doing this less	I am remaining about the same		I am doing this more	I am doing this less	I am remaining about the same
Listening	☐	☐	☐	Withdrawing from conflict	☐	☐	☐
Acting firmly and kindly	☐	☐	☐	Using consequences	☐	☐	☐
Becoming consistent	☐	☐	☐	Stimulating self-reliance	☐	☐	☐
Encouraging	☐	☐	☐	Stimulating responsible decision making	☐	☐	☐
Practicing mutual respect	☐	☐	☐				
Communicating love	☐	☐	☐	Taking time for fun	☐	☐	☐

I learned:

I plan to change my behavior by:

CHAPTER 2

Understanding More about Your Child and about Yourself as a Parent

In Chapter 1, you learned that people are social beings whose main goal in life is to belong. You discovered that children who misbehave are discouraged; they do not believe they can belong in useful ways. Their misbehavior is for the purpose of attention, power, revenge, or display of inadequacy. By choosing one or more of these four goals, children believe they can become significant; they can belong.

Now we take you a step further. We will consider three topics: Emotions, Life-Style, and The "Good" Parent. Each of these will add to your understanding of the relationship between you and your child.

Emotions

Emotions are, of course, a necessary aspect of our makeup. Consider what life would be without them. Although there would be no sorrow and no conflict, there would also be no joy, closeness, or love. Like a world without color, life would be dull without emotions.

Where do emotions come from? Why do we feel elated, angry, or annoyed? Why are some of us better at handling our emotions than others? If I'm not supposed to get angry with my children, what should I do with my anger?

Typically, we regard emotions as magical forces which invade us from the outside. We exclaim, "He made me so angry!" or "She's going to drive me crazy!" We seem not to realize that each of us is responsible for her or his own emotions.

Let's review our understanding of the motivation of human beings: that all behavior, including misbehavior, serves a purpose. Our emotions, too, are based on our beliefs and purposes. WE FEEL AS WE BELIEVE. If we believe that people are friendly and trustworthy, we create positive feelings to bring ourselves close to other people. If we believe that people are unfriendly and untrustworthy, we create hostile feelings to keep them away.

Parents often become annoyed and angry with children because the children will not do what the parents want them to. These hostile feelings of anger and annoyance serve the purpose of controlling the children. Once parents decide that they do not need to be controlling (i.e., that they can set limits and let the children decide and learn from the consequences), then there is no purpose for becoming annoyed and angry. You will learn more about how to set limits in a democratic fashion as this course proceeds.

Children learn to use their emotions to achieve one or more of the four goals. For example, consider the children who have discovered the power that exists in tears: They may use tears to get their own way or to be excused from facing reality. The use of tears may be a form of "water power." Consider "sensitive" children: They

wear their hurt feelings on their sleeves. Their lips tremble, their eyes become teary, their chins touch their chests. They seem to be wearing a sign which says, "Fragile — Handle with Care, or I'll Break." Their parents tend to believe these children are weak and need protection: "I have to be very careful with Danny; he's so easily hurt."

What the parents don't realize is that children such as Danny are far from weak or fragile. They are very powerful! They are using their feelings to force others to treat them as special. Their "sensitivity" often prompts others — especially their peers — to be hard on them. Then they feel justified in feeling even more sorry for themselves. Their self-pity in turn influences parents to come to their rescue; to treat them as special again. Thus, by being "sensitive" and getting themselves hurt, these children set themselves up to get paid off twice: (1) Their peers treat them as special by singling them out to pick on (not exactly the way they *want* to be treated, but it's better than being ignored), and (2) sympathetic adults try to "make it up" by treating them in special ways.

Sometimes parents lose patience with sensitive children. Then the children really make their

parents pay! They put on their best display of hurt feelings. Their parents feel guilty and attempt to make up for the wrongs. Remember, though, that children are often *not aware* of their purposes.

Once parents recognize how children can use emotions to manipulate adults, they are in a position to influence their children. Parents can get out of the vicious cycle by refraining from reacting when children try to use emotions to manipulate them. We know that becoming responsible for one's own feelings is a necessary part of growing up.

Life-Style

Beginning in the earliest days of our lives, we develop beliefs about who we are, who and what other people are, what is important in life, and how we should function so that we can belong. We live by our beliefs; they characterize our life-style.

Yet, our basic beliefs are often faulty. Why? Because our interpretations of our experiences are often inaccurate. We formed our most basic beliefs when we were very young. At that time, our limited experience caused us to misjudge and overgeneralize. Even as infants, we were forming the biased opinions and beliefs which now guide our lives.

It is important to understand the factors which contribute to the formation of our children's life-style. Once we are aware of these components, we are in a better position to influence our children positively.

Four major factors influence the children's life-style (as they have influenced our own). These factors are:

Family Atmosphere and Values

The pattern of human relationships set by parents is called the "family atmosphere." The atmosphere may be competitive or cooperative, friendly or hostile, autocratic or permissive, orderly or chaotic. The family atmosphere provides a model of human relationships for children.

Family values often account for similarities among children. If the parents or children are athletic, musical, or academically talented, these interests may become family values.

Family members can recognize some of their values while remaining unaware of others. Money, accumulating goods, hard work, and education are values easily recognized; power, control, winning, and being right are values often unrecognized.

Children cannot remain neutral about values their family holds; each must decide how to respond. For example, in a family in which religion is strongly valued, one child may embrace the faith while another rebels and becomes a doubter.

Nor do both parents have to agree on a belief before it can become a family value. For example, Mother may believe a college education is necessary for the children while Father believes college to be a waste of time. In a family with divided beliefs, each child must decide who to agree with and whose ideas to reject.

Sex Roles

The sex roles played by parents are guidelines for their children. From Father and Mother, children see what the roles of men and women are considered to be. Children base their attitudes toward their own sex and the opposite sex on their observations of their parents. They may accept or reject the models their parents present.

Family Constellation

The psychological position of a child in a family is often related to the child's position among siblings — first-born, second-born, etc.

Each child has a different position in the family and perceives all events from her or his own viewpoint. Thus, the family atmosphere accounts for similarities in traits, and the family constellation influences the differences among children. The oldest child sees things differently from the way the baby of the family sees them.

Competition between siblings is another important influence on personality development. As a result of competition, where one child succeeds, another becomes discouraged or fails. *A child is usually influenced most strongly by the sibling who differs most from himself.* Intense competition with this sibling influences personality formation.

In studying your own family, note the position of each child — eldest, second, middle, youngest, or only child. Each position tends to have its own characteristic line of development and related beliefs and attitudes. More important, try to understand the *psychological position* of each of your children. Some first-born children cannot hold off the challenge to the position they occupy; some last-born children refuse to be the baby. If a child is the first boy after a number of girls, or if the oldest child is a girl in a family which values boys, these psychological positions influence their treatment, hence, their viewpoints. The difference in ages between children also affects each child's psychological position. In a family in which the children are 15, 13, 12, and 6 years, the youngest tends to be regarded as an only child.

The place of children in the family can generally be described by the following characteristics:

The *first-born* is, for a while, an only child. This child receives considerable attention, but then — as the second child arrives — is suddenly dethroned. The child continues to want to be first, and strives to maintain that position. When the first child cannot maintain supremacy through positive behavior, he or she may try to get recognition in some other way.

The *second-born* is confronted with someone who is always ahead. This child may feel inadequate because of inability to keep up with the older sibling. The child may try to seek a place by becoming more of what the older children are not — becoming more aggressive or more passive, more dependent, more social or more self-sufficient.

If a third child enters the family, the second child becomes a middle child. The *middle child* frequently feels squeezed out, deprived of the rights and privileges of the oldest and of the baby. The middle child may come to believe that life is unfair, or may decide to overcome the "disadvantaged" position. This child tends to be overconcerned with fairness and sticking to the rules.

The *youngest child,* as the baby of the family, may appear to be at a disadvantage, but can become a tyrant. The youngest child is inclined to take advantage of the position: by being cutest, most pleasant, weakest, or most awkward — all positions from which he or she can demand service. The youngest child may seek a place by becoming a clown or by openly rebelling.

The *only child* lives the formative years among persons who are bigger and more capable. Only children tend to develop a distinctive style which ensures them a place with adults; they may become very verbal, charming, and intelligent, or — if it suits their purpose — shy and helpless. They may also feel they are special and entitled to have their own way.

It is important to recognize that these positions in the family constellation only *influence* an individual's personality development; they do not directly determine it. Each individual makes his or her own decisions.

Methods of Training

Another important factor influencing children's life-styles is the parents' attitude and behavior toward children and toward themselves. Parents may be consistently autocratic, permissive, or democratic, or they may be inconsistent and fluctuate between these attitudes and behaviors. Fathers and mothers may basically agree or disagree on child-training procedures.

Our own rearing influences our present behavior as parents. For example: If we have been brought up to believe that we must be best, we may push our children as symbols of our desired status in the community. If we believe that we are entitled to have our own way, we may try to force our children to cater to our wishes or to expect others to cater to theirs. However, the results of our training are not always what we expect, because it is the child, not the parents, who decides how the child will respond.

In response to these four major influences (Family Atmosphere and Values, Sex Roles, Family Constellation, and Methods of Training) children develop their convictions and long-range goals. If they are able to meet their immediate goals through constructive acts, they become cooperative children. If, however, they find that they cannot achieve their goals constructively, they may become discouraged children who feel they must misbehave to secure a place in life.

MISBEHAVING CHILDREN ARE DISCOURAGED CHILDREN. They are expressing feelings of inadequacy. They lack feelings of belonging and are continually striving for status. They choose one or more of the four goals of misbehavior to achieve significance. For example: A boy wants always to be first. He becomes discouraged. He may still try to be first, by seeking attention — by becoming the best at getting others to notice. Or, he may try to become the most powerful person in his family, or the best at gaining revenge. Or, he may decide to give up and display his inadequacy. Misbehaving children may be active or passive, or they may make a pretense of good behavior which, in reality, is destructive. For example, some discouraged children display "good" behavior to gain advantage over others.

The "Good" Parent

One of the greatest handicaps a child can suffer is to be raised by a "Good" Parent. "Good" Parents are those who are so involved with their children that they believe they must do everything for the children.

"Good" Parents may become servants to their children. They make sure that the youngsters get up on time and dress properly. They are continually admonishing them: "Be a good boy," "Button your coat," "Remember your books," "Polish your shoes," etc. They leave no stone unturned as they "snoopervise" the children's every move. A child's return from school brings on a new wave of concern: "How did you do today?" "Let me see your school papers," "Change your clothes," "Eat your supper," "Hurry up and get to bed."

"Good" Parents are usually well intentioned. Nevertheless, their behavior robs their children of self-confidence and independence. "Good" Parents assume responsibility for everything their children do, believing that their children's behavior reflects on their competence as parents. Concerned with their images in the community, they take on their children's responsibilities (so that the children will "Turn out right"). They do this instead of respecting the children by letting them learn from experience. They pity and protect their youngsters from all consequences and prevent them from learning on their own. Keep-

ing their children dependent helps them feel important. "Good" Parents have a lot of help in maintaining their roles. Our society holds such unrealistic expectations that it is difficult for parents to be secure in their roles. A society which is overconcerned with mistakes is expert in discouraging its members.

If we believe in the democratic approach to parenthood and seek to treat our children as equals, we must allow them to make decisions and experience the consequences, either positive or negative (dangerous situations excepted, of course). We must also trust them to be able to learn from their experiences.

"Good" Parents deny their children opportunities to learn the concept of mutual respect. Whenever parents control, dominate, overprotect, or pity, they are violating respect for their child. Whenever they allow themselves to be "doormats," they are violating respect for themselves. In either case, they are neglecting to train their children to respect the rights of others.

To teach a child mutual respect, parents need to be firm without being domineering. This implies that they be firm with their own rights, yet refrain from depriving children of theirs. For example: Gus and his friend are throwing a softball in the family room. Mother intercepts the soft-

ball, saying, "I'm sorry, boys, but the softball could break something. You may play something else or play catch outside. Which would you rather do?"

Mother's calm statement of fact establishes her rights — to live in an undamaged home — while it respects the boys by allowing them to choose an acceptable activity.

Mary is always misplacing things. Instead of finding the things for her or helping her search, Mother and Father can allow Mary to decide whether to place her things in the proper place or to experience the inconvenience of not having the item.

In contrast to "Good" Parents, Responsible Parents, such as the ones in these examples, are more concerned with building their children's feelings of responsibility and self-confidence than in protecting their own image in the community. Responsible Parents give their children choices and let them experience the results of their decisions.

QUESTIONS

1. Do you ever use your emotions to influence other people? How?

2. How do children use emotions in negative ways?

3. What did you learn about sensitive children?

4. In general, how can we behave effectively when children are using their feelings in order to accomplish one of the goals of misbehavior?

5. What is meant by "life-style"?
   a. Why are our beliefs about ourselves and others often faulty?
   b. What are the four major factors which influence a person's life-style?
   c. What is meant by: family atmosphere? values? sex roles? family constellation? methods of training?

6. What tend to be the characteristics of the first child? second child? middle child? youngest child? only child?

7. Can you see the influence of the family constellation on your own children? In what ways?

8. What do the authors mean by the "Good" Parent? How does a "Good" Parent behave?

9. Why do "Good" Parents behave as they do? What are the consequences for their children?

10. What is meant by the Responsible Parent? How do Responsible Parents behave? What are the consequences for their children?

PROBLEM SITUATION

Mr. and Mrs. Brown disagree on child-training procedures. Mr. Brown is strict and believes that their daughter, Alice, should "toe the line." Mrs. Brown believes in democratic procedures. Whenever Mr. Brown disagrees with his wife's methods, he interferes in front of Alice, and an argument develops. Mrs. Brown also interferes with her husband's disciplinary methods.

1. What are both Mr. and Mrs. Brown trying to prove?
2. What are the consequences of these faulty beliefs?
3. What is Alice learning?
4. How is this affecting the formation of her life-style?
5. If either Mr. or Mrs. Brown asked you for advice, what would you say?

ACTIVITY FOR THE WEEK

1. Analyze your children's emotional displays in terms of the four goals of misbehavior and use what you have learned in this session to influence your children.
2. Watch for a situation in which you are trapped — or nearly trapped — into being the "Good" Parent. Take steps to avoid it or to avoid its happening again.

CHART 2

Differences between the "Good" Parent and the Responsible Parent

"GOOD" PARENT

Parent's Belief	Possible Parent Behaviors	Possible Results for Child
I must control.	Demands obedience. Rewards and punishes. Tries to win. Insists parent is right and child is wrong.	Rebels — must win or be right. Hides true feelings. Feels anxious. Seeks revenge; feels life is unfair. Gives up. Evades, lies, steals. Lacks self-discipline.
I am superior.	Pities child. Takes responsibility. Overprotects. Acts self-righteous. Spoils child. Shames child.	Learns to pity self and to blame others. Criticizes others. Feels life is unfair. Feels inadequate. Expects others to give. Feels need to be superior.
I am entitled. You owe me.	Is overconcerned with fairness. Gives with strings attached.	Doesn't trust others. Feels life is unfair. Feels exploited. Learns to exploit others.
I must be perfect.	Demands perfection from all. Finds fault. Is overconcerned about what others think; pushes child to make self look good.	Believes he/she is never good enough. Becomes perfectionistic. Feels discouraged. Worries about others' opinions.
I don't count. Others are more important than I.	Overindulges child. Becomes "slave." Gives in to child's demands. Feels guilty about saying no.	Expects to receive. Has poor social relationships. Does not respect rights of others. Is selfish.

RESPONSIBLE PARENT

Parent's Belief	Possible Parent Behaviors	Possible Results for Child
I believe the child can make decisions.	Permits choices. Encourages.	Feels self-confident; tries. Contributes. Cooperates. Solves problems. Becomes resourceful.
I am equal, not more or less worthwhile than others.	Believes in and respects child. Encourages independence. Gives choices and responsibility. Expects child to contribute.	Develops self-reliance and responsibility. Learns to make decisions. Respects self and others. Believes in equality.
I believe in mutual respect.	Promotes equality. Encourages mutual respect. Avoids making child feel guilty.	Respects self and others. Has increased social feeling. Trusts others.
I am human; I have "courage to be imperfect."	Sets realistic standards. Focuses on strengths. Encourages. Is not concerned with own image. Is patient.	Focuses on task at hand, not on self-elevation. Sees mistakes as challenge to keep trying. Has courage to try new experiences. Is tolerant of others.
I believe all people are important, including myself.	Encourages mutual respect and contribution. Refuses to be "doormat." Knows when to say no.	Has good social relationships. Respects the rights of others. Is generous.

Understanding Your Child and Yourself

1. Emotions serve a purpose. Our emotions always support our real intentions.

2. Our feelings don't "just happen." We bring them about.

3. Our feelings are influenced by our beliefs.

4. "Sensitive" children try to force us to treat them as special.

5. Emotions can be used to control and retaliate against others, or to protect and excuse ourselves from functioning.

6. You are responsible for your own feelings and behavior.

7. A feeling of competition between brothers and sisters discourages certain traits and stimulates the development of others.

8. The child's position in the family constellation influences but does not determine personality and behavior. In the final analysis, each individual makes his or her own decisions.

9. Misbehaving children are discouraged children.

10. "Good" Parents are so involved with their children that they believe they must do everything for them.

11. Avoid "snoopervising" the child's every move.

12. "Good" Parents rob children of self-confidence and independence.

13. When you protect children from the consequences of their behavior, you are preventing them from learning.

14. Responsible parents give children choices and let them experience the results of their decisions.

15. Be kind; show respect for your child. Be firm; show respect for yourself.

16. Setting high goals and placing a premium on being best will influence your child to give up if she or he cannot be the best.

17. Pity tells a child you believe he or she is incapable.

18. Children display inadequacy in order to be excused or to get special service.

19. It is in the best interests of children to help them become responsible.

20. Controlling, dominating, overprotecting and pitying all violate respect for the child.

My Plan for Improving Relationships

(An opportunity to assess progress each week)

My specific concern:

My usual response:

☐ talking, lecturing   ☐ punishing, removing privileges, shaming

☐ noticing, nagging   ☐ threatening, warning

☐ becoming angry   ☐ other_____

My progress this week:

	I am doing this more	I am doing this less	I am remaining about the same		I am doing this more	I am doing this less	I am remaining about the same
Listening	☐	☐	☐	Withdrawing from conflict	☐	☐	☐
Acting firmly and kindly	☐	☐	☐	Using consequences	☐	☐	☐
Becoming consistent	☐	☐	☐	Stimulating self-reliance	☐	☐	☐
Encouraging	☐	☐	☐	Stimulating responsible decision making	☐	☐	☐
Practicing mutual respect	☐	☐	☐				
Communicating love	☐	☐	☐	Taking time for fun	☐	☐	☐

I learned:

I plan to change my behavior by:

CHAPTER 3

Encouragement: Building Your Child's Confidence and Feelings of Worth

One of the most important skills for improving the relationship between parents and children is encouragement. Encouragement is the process whereby you focus on the assets and strengths of your children to build their self-confidence and self-esteem. Encouragement helps your children believe in themselves and their abilities. Parents who encourage help their children accept and learn from mistakes; they help their children develop the courage to be imperfect.

In autocratic households, children receive their sense of worth by accepting rewards and punishments from those in positions of power. In democratic households, children are influenced by encouragement.

Helping your children build their feelings of self-esteem may require you to change your usual communication and behavior patterns. Instead of focusing on the children's mistakes, point out what they do that you like or appreciate. This will require you to change to a positive approach.

We all want the best for our children. But while our intentions are honorable, our methods for helping our children grow responsible often fall short of the desired results. In the following statements, consider the difference between our ideals and what we actually do. As you read, be thinking of actions that would be more consistent with the ideals.

Our ideal:	What we really do:
My child should be responsible and independent.	Force child to perform; do child's work.
My child should be respectful and courteous.	Talk down to child; criticize, distrust, lecture, and punish child.
My child should be happy.	Compliment success, but dwell on mistakes; tell child he or she can do better.
My child should have concern for others.	Show lack of concern for child by lecturing, reprimanding, scolding, shaming, using child as servant, talking down, giving in at the expense of our own rights.
My child should love me.	Demand affection, but reject child when we're "too busy."
My child should feel adequate, be courageous, and feel good about himself or herself.	Do too much for child, implying child is not capable; criticize, make fun of, refuse to allow child to try difficult tasks.

Often our day-to-day relationships with our children do not match our honorable intentions and ideals — and there is reason for this. Our society has influenced us to be expert at finding fault, to expect the worst, and, in general, to be discouraging toward ourselves and our children. But we don't *have* to perpetuate this discouraging cycle. We can replace our "programming" with a new set of attitudes and behaviors.

Let's consider parents who have decided to become more encouraging. First, they plan to eliminate the following attitudes and behaviors:

Negative Expectations

The most powerful forces in human relationships are *expectations*. Our expectations are communicated by word and gesture. Children internalize the expectations of adults; that is, they take them for their own. For example: When we believe a child won't succeed at a difficult task, we communicate that belief one way or another. The child begins to doubt his or her ability to do the task and behaves in the manner we expect: the child fails.

Unreasonably High Standards

We often set standards which are impossible for our children to meet. We expect their rooms to be "neat as a pin." Every hair on their heads must be in place. They must do well in endeavors which are important to us — schoolwork, athletics, chores, etc. We communicate that we expect them to do better, and let them know that whatever they do, it's never as good as it could have been. We expect performance beyond their ages and abilities.

Promoting Competition between Brothers and Sisters

We are usually unaware of promoting competition between our children. We praise the successful child while we ignore or criticize the unsuccessful child. Comparisons may be expressed nonverbally: a gesture or a facial expression can trigger competition as effectively as a comment. Competition between siblings has an effect on the strengths as well as on the deficiencies of the individual. A child often becomes good at something a brother or sister cannot do well. The same child may decide not to try things which a brother or sister does well, because the child feels he or she cannot succeed.

For example: Ten-year-old Joan is well behaved, a good student in school, and a responsible helper at home. Her seven-year-old brother, Randy, does poorly in school and is generally uncooperative there and at home. Joan and Randy's parents are obviously proud of their daughter's accomplishments and disappointed in their son. It is possible that Joan is maintaining her favored position at Randy's expense. One can guess who tattles on Randy when he misbehaves. For Joan to continue to be the "apple of her parent's eye," Randy must continue to be the "black sheep." If Randy were to become more cooperative and responsible, Joan's place as the "good" child would be threatened. Chances are, her behavior would change: she would begin to adopt a role as the "bad" child in an effort to reestablish a place in the family.

At this point you may be thinking, "You mean when I succeed in helping my 'problem' child, my 'good' child will become a problem?" Yes. This is usually what happens. In fact, since the children are competitive, a role switch typically occurs before permanent change sets in. But don't despair. The switch to "problem" behavior is usually only temporary. As you continue to work in encouraging ways with *all* your children, you will be decreasing the competition. The children will become more cooperative and less prone to try to establish a place at the expense of each other.

Overambition

Overambitious parents want to be the best possible parents. To accomplish this, they insist that their children also demonstrate excellence. Their attitude may influence the children not to try anything unless they are certain they will be tops, with the result that they avoid areas in which they see possible failure. In overambitious families, both parents and children lack the courage to be imperfect.

On the other hand, some parents become very concerned when children participate only if they can be best. These parents may outwardly wish their children did not have this attitude, yet make comments such as, "You could do better if you would . . ." or "Keep up the good work." Such comments imply that the children are worthwhile only when they succeed. Thus the ambitious parent communicates that the child is not quite good enough.

Double Standards

Many parents believe that they should have rights and privileges which they deny to their children. Mom tells the children to pick up their belongings, yet clutters the living room with papers brought home from work. Father complains that he works hard all day and should not be required to do household chores, yet he demands that the children do chores after school. (He forgets that school and play are children's work and that they are just as uninterested in doing chores as he is.)

Children recognize that certain socially prescribed rights and privileges, such as driving a car, are restricted to age. But when parents assume other rights and privileges and deny them to children, this tells the children that they are of less value in the family.

Parents who want to overcome these discouraging attitudes and, instead, encourage their children must be willing to *work toward the following attitudes:*

Accept Your Children as They Are, Not Only as They Could Be

If we want our children to see themselves as worthwhile persons, we must genuinely accept them as they are, with all of their imperfections. Many parents believe that the way to help children improve is to dwell on their shortcomings. Actually, this approach has just the opposite effect: children become discouraged. Imagine what it would be like for you to be constantly reminded of your faults. Would you feel worthwhile? Of course there is room for improvement in all of us, but that is not the point here. The point is that people cannot improve unless they feel good enough about themselves to believe they can improve. Imagine how it would feel to receive frequent encouragement and to know that you are valued by your family.

We believe that we value our children, and sometimes we tell them so. But our actions often contradict our words. We tell our children they are wonderful and then act dissatisfied when they do not live up to our standards.

We must learn to *separate the deed from the doer.* Children will not always perform as we would like. We must let them know that they are valued as persons no matter how they perform. Beth missed five words out of twenty on a spelling test. Instead of dwelling on the five errors, the parent could point out the fifteen words that are spelled correctly. Focusing on the positive gives Beth the feeling that she is OK.

She is well aware of the five errors; there is no need to point them out. Accepting Beth *as she is* helps her feel worthwhile as a person and gives her the courage to try.

Ignore Tattling

Paying attention to tattling has a very discouraging effect. Children use tattling to make themselves look good or to get even. Tattlers achieve their purpose by using the ultimate weapon: the parents. They are successful when the culprit gets caught. When parents allow themselves to be used in this manner, they are also inviting the "victim" to use them at the next opportunity.

Parents sometimes try to stop tattling by explaining that they are no longer interested in tattletales. Although this approach may seem sensible, the effect is not, for the child still gains attention for tattling. It's best to ignore the tattling by busying oneself with other things. While we believe an effective way for dealing with many misbehaviors is to ignore them, we wish to emphasize that ignoring negative behavior must be accompanied by giving attention for positive behavior.

Some parents are reluctant to put a stop to tattling. They fear that their children won't tell them when someone is doing something harmful. We haven't found this to be true. Children know the difference between tattling and informing parents when someone is doing something harmful.

If a child is involved in something dangerous, keep this principle in mind: *Deal with the situation, not with the offender.* Otherwise, the dangerous act may be repeated as a way to get you involved.

Be Positive

After parents recognize how certain beliefs and attitudes hinder their attempts to encourage their children, they must also become aware of what behavior interferes with their intentions.

First of all, an encouraging parent stops using negative comments about a child. When problems arise, the encouraging parent uses methods which are based on respect for the child — listening, I-messages, problem solving, and natural and logical consequences. You will learn about these methods later on.

Avoid the temptation to interfere when your child is trying to work through a problem or perform a task. Interference communicates a hidden criticism: "You aren't able to do that correctly." If your child asks for help, keep your comments in the form of suggestions, not formulas: "What do you think would happen if . . . ?" "Have you considered . . . ?" "I've found it helpful to . . ."

If your children request help in order to gain attention or to get out of thinking or working independently, tell them you have confidence in their ability: "You were able to do ＿＿ before, so you can handle this."

Have Faith in Children So They May Believe in Themselves

Few children will learn to believe in themselves if their parents do not believe in them. We must learn to play down our children's mistakes and to communicate our confidence instead. We must be alert to point out the positive aspects of their efforts.

Focus on Contributions, Assets, and Strengths

To feel adequate, children must feel useful and know that their contributions count.

Help your children feel useful by identifying their talents and suggesting ways they might use these talents to contribute to the family. A child can gain a satisfying place in the family by contributing to it. For example, a child may be poor at dusting but good at sweeping the driveway. Mom and Dad can show the child how to use this ability to make life better for everyone in the family. They can do this not by flattery, but by sincerely commenting that the child's efforts really help and are appreciated.

Recognize Effort and Improvement As Well As Final Accomplishment

When parents hold out for achievement — a better grade in math, a neat room at home — some children conclude they are not good enough unless they approximate perfection. The child who has difficulty in math may never learn to multiply if the parent fails to notice his or her efforts to improve. Encouragement implies reasonable expectations (one step at a time) and that we accept the child's efforts and failures as well as successes.

Encourage Rather Than Praise

Many parents believe they are encouraging children when they praise them. They don't realize that *praise can be discouraging.* At first glance, praise and encouragement appear to be the same process. This is because both praise and encouragement focus on positive behaviors. To understand the very important differences, consider the *purpose* and *effect* of praise, versus encouragement.

Praise is a type of reward. It is based on competition; it is given for winning and being the best. In effect, the parent who praises is saying, "If you do something I consider good, you will have the reward of being recognized and valued by me." Praise is an attempt to motivate children with external rewards.

Encouragement, on the other hand, is given for effort or for improvement, however slight. It focuses on the child's assets and strengths as a means for him or her to contribute to the good of all. The parent who encourages is not interested in how the child compares with others. Instead, the parent cares about the child's accepting herself or himself and developing the courage to face difficult tasks. Encouragement is aimed at helping a child feel worthy. Thus, it attempts to motivate children through internal means. Also, unlike praise, encouragement can be given at a time when children are "down" — when they feel they are not doing well enough or when they are facing failure.

Praise, like punishment, is a method of social control. Over-reliance on praise can produce crippling effects. Children come to believe their worth depends upon the opinions of others. The conforming child who holds this belief is usually successful in earning praise. In turn, praise may be discouraging to the conforming child. He or she may be willing to cooperate only if praised; if not praised, the child may stop contributing. Also, believing "I am worthwhile only when I please others" may influence children to make decisions which are detrimental to themselves.

Discouraged children who hold this belief seldom perform up to adult standards; therefore, they seldom receive praise. On rare occasion, such children may earn praise; however, when the reward comes, their behavior may suddenly become worse than it was before, for the following reasons:

1. They do not believe they are worthy of praise, and feel a need to prove how unworthy they are.

2. They fear they can never earn praise again. In effect, they wonder, "What can I do for an encore? I'd better save face by not trying."

Thus, praise for the child who is discouraged and desperately needs recognition can have the effect of discouraging the child even more.

Some children resent authority figures. When parents attempt to control such children through praise, the children refuse to repeat the desired behavior. They feel "put down" and refuse cooperation, viewing any form of it as giving in. Some misbehave shortly after being praised in a further attempt to defeat the controlling parent. Confused, the praising parent often uses punishment in an effort to regain control. Thus, the vicious cycle continues: praise (or some other type of reward) . . . and punish . . . praise . . . and punish . . .

In following chapters we will deal with alternatives to punishment. First, we want to make certain you understand the concept of encouragement and how it differs from praise.

Praise employs words which place *value judgments* on the child.

Examples:

"You're such a good boy!" or, **"Good girl!"**

This is not an easy expectation to live up to — "Am I supposed to be good all the time?" "Am

I really good?" "Am I good even when I'm not doing what they want?" In contrast, encouragement focuses on how the child's contribution helped.

"You got an A! That's great!"

Great for whom? Is it great because it makes you feel like a "Good" Parent? Is the child to infer that he or she is worthwhile only when the grade is A? What would you have said if the child had come home with a C? In contrast, encouragement focuses on how the child feels about the A — "You seem pretty proud of that A."

"What a good job you did!"

While you may think it's good, are you sure the child agrees? Besides, whose evaluation is more important: yours, or the child's? In contrast, encouragement would help the child feel worthwhile by letting him or her know that the contribution was appreciated.

"I'm so proud of you!"

Could it be that you are really saying, "You make me look so good," or, "You really pleased me, because you're doing what I want"? In contrast, encouragement would focus on how the child feels about the noteworthy performance.

Such words of praise focus on external evaluation and self-elevation. Praising behavior on the part of parents teaches children to compare themselves with others and to work for personal gain only.

Encouragement focuses instead on internal evaluation and contributions. Encouraging parents teach their children to accept their own inadequacies, to have confidence in themselves, and to feel useful through contribution.

Chart 3 sums up the differences between praise and encouragement.

The Special Language of Encouragement

When comments about children's efforts are in order, we must be very careful not to place value judgments on what they have done. Too often, we make positive comments in a praising manner. Such comments express our values and opinions, rather than help children believe in themselves.

Be alert to eliminate value-loaded words from your vocabulary at these moments (for example, good, great, excellent, etc.). Substitute words of praise with phrases which express the special meaning of encouragement:

Phrases that demonstrate acceptance:

"I like the way you handled that."
"I like the way you tackle a problem."
"I'm glad you enjoy learning."
"I'm glad you're pleased with it."
"Since you're not satisfied, what do you think you can do so that you will be pleased with it?"
"It looks as if you enjoyed that."
"How do you feel about it?"

Phrases that show confidence:

"Knowing you, I'm sure you'll do fine."
"You'll make it!"
"I have confidence in your judgment."
"That's a rough one, but I'm sure you'll work it out."
"You'll figure it out."

Phrases that focus on contributions, assets, and appreciation:

"Thanks; that helped a lot."
"It was thoughtful of you to_____."
"Thanks, I really appreciate_____, because it makes my job much easier."
"I need your help on_____."
To a family group: "I really enjoyed today. Thanks."
"You have skill in_____. Would you do that for the family?"

Phrases that recognize effort and improvement:

"It looks as if you really worked hard on that."
"It looks as if you spent a lot of time thinking that through."

"I see that you're moving along."
"Look at the progress you've made."
(be specific; tell how)
"You're improving in . . ." (be specific)
"You may not feel that you've reached your goal, but look how far you've come!"

A Word of Caution:

Encouraging words can become discouraging if motivated by a parent's desire to establish "good" behavior permanently or by an "I told you so" attitude. Avoid giving with one hand and taking away with the other; that is, avoid qualifying or moralizing comments.

For example:
"It looks as if you really worked hard on that;
. . . so, why not do that all the time?"
. . . it's about time."
. . . see what you can do when you try!"
In summary, encouragement is:
Valuing and accepting children as they are (not putting conditions on acceptance).
Pointing out the positive aspects of behavior.
Showing faith in children so that they can come to believe in themselves.
Recognizing effort and improvement (rather than requiring achievement).
Showing appreciation for contributions.

QUESTIONS

1. What is meant by "encouragement"? How does encouragement affect a child's feeling about himself or herself?
2. How can negative expectations lead to poor performances?
3. What effects can the imposition of unreasonably high standards have on children?
4. How does reinforcing competition between brothers and sisters usually affect them?
5. What can be the results of overambition?
6. How do double standards affect the relationship between parents and children?
7. What is the meaning of "Accept your children as they are, not only as they could be"? Why is this important?
8. How does your attention to tattling give a discouraging message to the one who tattles, as well as the one who is tattled on?

9. What is the difference between praise and encouragement? Why is praise often inappropriate and ineffective?
10. How are the examples of "The Special Language of Encouragement" different from words of praise?
11. Why is it important to recognize effort and improvement as well as accomplishment?
12. What are some ways you could encourage your child? (Ask for specific examples.)
13. In the comparisons between our ideals and what we really do, which statements do you feel characterize your relationships with your children?

EXERCISE

The following situations require encouragement. How would you respond?
Write what you would do or say when:

1. Your daughter complains that the arithmetic homework is too difficult.
2. Your son has attempted to dress himself; his shirt is on backward, his shoes are on the wrong feet, etc.
3. Your son has just helped you clean the kitchen.
4. Your son is worried that he will not do well in a music recital.
5. Your daughter returns from an athletic contest after playing well but having lost.

PROBLEM SITUATION

Your daughter's class held an election today. She was nominated along with two other students for class president. She lost the election and is very discouraged.

1. What might she believe about herself?
2. How would you encourage her?

ACTIVITY FOR THE WEEK

This week, find ways to encourage your children. In each instance, notice what happened, how you encouraged the child, and the child's response.

CHART 3

Differences between Praise and Encouragement

PRAISE

Underlying Character-istics	Message Sent to Child	Possible Results
1. Focus is on external control.	"You are worth-while only when you do what I want." "You cannot and should not be trusted."	Child learns to measure worth by ability to conform; or, child rebels (views any form of cooperation as giving in).
2. Focus is on external evaluation.	"To be worth-while you must please me." "Please or Perish."	Child learns to measure worth on how well he/she pleases others. Child learns to fear disapproval.
3. Is rewarded only for well-done, completed tasks.	"To be worth-while you must meet my standards."	Child develops unrealistic standards and learns to measure worth by how closely she/he reaches perfection. Child learns to dread failure.
4. Focuses on self-elevation and personal gain.	"You're the best. You must remain superior to others to be worthwhile."	Child learns to be overcompetitive, to get ahead at the expense of others. Feels worthwhile only when "on top."

ENCOURAGEMENT

Underlying Character-istics	Message Sent to Child	Possible Results
Focus is on child's ability to manage life constructively.	"I trust you to become responsible and independent."	Child learns courage to be imperfect and willingness to try. Child gains self-confidence and comes to feel responsible for own behavior.
Focus is on internal evaluation.	"How you feel about yourself and your own efforts is most important."	Child learns to evaluate own progress and to make own decisions.
Recognizes effort and improvement.	"You don't have to be perfect. Effort and improvement are important."	Child learns to accept efforts of self and others. Child develops desire to stay with tasks (persistence).
Focuses on assets, contributions, and appreciation.	"Your contribution counts. We function better with you. We appreciate what you have done."	Child learns to use talents and efforts for good of all, not only for personal gain. Child learns to feel glad for successes of others as well as for own successes.

POINTS TO REMEMBER

Encouragement: Building Your Child's Confidence and Feelings of Worth

1. Encouragement is the process of focusing on your children's assets and strengths in order to build their self-confidence and feelings of worth.

2. Focus on what is good about the child or the situation. See the positive.

3. Accept your children as they are. Don't make your love and acceptance dependent on their behavior.

4. Have faith in your children so they can come to believe in themselves.

5. Let your children know their worth. Recognize improvement and effort, not just accomplishment.

6. Respect your children. It will lay the foundation of their self-respect.

7. Praise is reserved for things well done. It implies a spirit of competition. Encouragement is given for effort or improvement. It implies a spirit of cooperation.

8. The most powerful forces in human relationships are expectations. We can influence a person's behavior by changing our expectations of the person.

9. Lack of faith in children helps them to anticipate failure.

10. Standards that are too high invite failure and discouragement.

11. Avoid subtle encouragement of competition between brothers and sisters.

12. Avoid using discouraging words and actions.

13. Avoid tacking qualifiers to your words of encouragement. Don't "give with one hand and take away with the other."

14. The sounds of encouragement are words that build feelings of adequacy:

"I like the way you handled that."

"I know you can handle it."

"I appreciate what you did."

"It looks as if you worked very hard on that."

"You're improving."

Be generous with them.

My Plan for
Improving Relationships

(An opportunity to assess progress each week)

My specific concern:

My usual response:

☐ talking, lecturing   ☐ punishing, removing privileges, shaming

☐ noticing, nagging   ☐ threatening, warning

☐ becoming angry   ☐ other_____

My progress this week:

	I am doing this more	I am doing this less	I am remaining about the same		I am doing this more	I am doing this less	I am remaining about the same
Listening	☐	☐	☐	Withdrawing from conflict	☐	☐	☐
Acting firmly and kindly	☐	☐	☐	Using consequences	☐	☐	☐
Becoming consistent	☐	☐	☐	Stimulating self-reliance	☐	☐	☐
Encouraging	☐	☐	☐	Stimulating responsible decision making	☐	☐	☐
Practicing mutual respect	☐	☐	☐				
Communicating love	☐	☐	☐	Taking time for fun	☐	☐	☐

I learned:

I plan to change my behavior by:

CHAPTER 4

Communication: How to Listen to Your Child

To maintain a satisfying relationship with your child, you must communicate effectively.

This chapter and the next will cover your ability to listen to your children. To make it easier for your children to communicate with you, your communication must convince your children that you care enough to listen.

Poor communication is the mode of life for many families.

"Do you talk with your child?"

"Sure, I talk to my child."

How much of this "talking to" consists of nagging, reminding, criticizing, cajoling, threatening, lecturing, questioning, advising, evaluating, probing, and ridiculing?

These tactics, however well meant, diminish, rather than improve, communication. They strain relationships. Imagine lecturing or criticizing your friends — and watching them flare up in anger, or make excuses to leave for home. If most parents treated their children the way they treat their friends, relationships with the children would improve. Conversely, if they treated their friends the way they treat their children, their friendships would surely deteriorate.

Think of the ways you want people to respond when you are upset. Sometimes you want to be left alone. At other times you want someone to listen and try to understand and accept your feelings. Is it possible that your child needs the same consideration?

Roles We Play When Children Express Their Feelings

Many of us have been taught that feelings of anger, disappointment, and fear are wrong and should not be expressed. Consequently, many of us do not know how to handle these feelings when our children express them. In our awkwardness, we respond in terms of roles:

Commander in Chief

The parent who plays this role is interested in keeping things well under control and demands that the child get rid of the negative feelings immediately and "shape up." *Orders, commands,* and *threats* are the tools the Commander uses to keep the upper hand.

The Moralist

The Moralist is a "shouldist!" "You should do this," "You shouldn't do that," *preaches* this parent. The Moralist is very concerned that the child have the "proper" feelings.

The Know-It-All

Parents who play this role try to show the child that adults have been traveling life's road for a long time and have accumulated most of its answers. These parents *lecture, advise, make appeals to the child's reason,* and try to show how *superior* they themselves are.

The Judge

These parents have already pronounced the child guilty without a trial. They are interested in proving that *they are always right* and that the *child is always wrong.*

The Critic

Like the Judge, the Moralist, and the Know-It-All, the parent playing this role is interested in being right. But The Critic relies on *ridicule, name-calling, sarcasm,* or *jokes* to put the child down.

The Psychologist

The Psychologist tries to analyze the problem. With the best of intentions, this parent wants to hear all the details — so that the parent will be in a better position to set the child straight. The Psychologist *diagnoses, analyzes,* and *questions.*

The Consoler

Parents who play this role attempt to excuse themselves from involvement by treating the child's feelings lightly. *Simple reassurance,* a *pat on the back,* and the *pretense* that all is well when it isn't are this parent's answer to a child's worries and anxieties.

While we are strong in our criticism of these roles, we wish to emphasize that the parents who play them do so not maliciously, but with the best of intentions.

Becoming an Effective Listener

The sort of communication we are aiming for is based upon mutual respect. "Mutual respect" means that children and parents allow each other to express their beliefs and feelings honestly, without fear of rejection. It means accepting what the other person says. You may not agree with your children, but you can demonstrate that you accept their feelings. You show acceptance through your tone and the words you use.

Becoming an effective listener requires concentration. It involves establishing eye contact and a posture which says, "I'm listening." Sometimes good listening requires us to be silent. Sometimes it requires us to respond.

Reflective Listening

Listening to our children requires letting them know that we recognize the feelings behind what they are saying and what they are not saying.

We know that a person who is upset tends to lose perspective. By listening reflectively, we can help a child think through an upsetting problem. That is, we can *reflect* and *clarify* the child's feelings to help lay a foundation for the child to resolve the problem. Here is an example of reflective listening:

Child: "That teacher is unfair! I'll never do well in that class!"

Parent: "You're feeling angry and disappointed, and you've given up."

Thus, reflective listening involves grasping what the child feels and means, and then stating this meaning so the child feels understood and accepted. *Reflective listening provides a sort of mirror for the child to see himself or herself more clearly.* In other words, it gives the child "feedback."

Communication between persons can be described in terms of *closed* and *open* responses. A closed response is the one which indicates that the listener has neither heard nor understood what was said. Closed responses tend to cut off communication.

In contrast, an open response is one which indicates that the listener has heard what the other person has said. An open response reflects the speaker's message in a way that clearly indicates the listener has heard the feelings behind the words.

Here are examples of closed and open responses following a child's remark:

Child: "I'm really disappointed with Billy and the other kids for not coming over to play with me. There's nothing to do."

Closed Response: "Well, things don't always go the way we want them to. That's part of life."

Open Response: "It seems as if no one cares, and you're feeling left out."

The first response does not accept the child's feelings; it says that what he or she feels doesn't matter. This type of put-down blocks communication and may leave the child feeling rejected.

The second response recognizes what the child is feeling. It shows acceptance and concern. The child may decide to tell you more.

Reflective listening means that we produce open responses which reflect the child's feelings and meanings. It requires sensitivity to a wide variety of feelings plus the ability to express them. It is nonjudgmental. Thus, it encourages the child to feel heard and to keep talking.

The communication process is always nonverbal as well as verbal. Our actions, facial expressions, and tone of voice communicate whether or not we are listening. We can communicate nonverbally through a smile, a frown, or a pat on the back. Silently deciding not to overprotect, nag, or interfere communicates acceptance. When we respond nonjudgmentally by accepting our child's feelings and meanings, both verbally and nonverbally, we strengthen empathy and communication.

It is helpful to use adverbs to communicate that you understand the intensity of the feeling being expressed. For example:

"You're *extremely* angry with Robert."

"You're *especially* excited about that campout."

"You're very sad about losing your friend."

Responding to Nonverbal Messages

One cannot catch the meaning of a sullen look, a broad smile, or a tearful face simply by listening. Behavior expresses meaning, sometimes more clearly than words. *One must learn to catch the meanings of a child's behavior by "tuning in" to more than his or her words.*

Examples of responding to nonverbal behavior are:

"Your frown seems to say that you disagree."

"When your face lights up that way, you look very happy."

"Looks as if you are really upset. Want to talk about it?"

Statements acknowledging nonverbal cues invite the child to express her or his feelings.

Typical Comments from Parents about Reflective Listening

Some parents, when first learning about reflective listening, are skeptical. Typical comments are, "Why say the child's words back to him?" "I don't like to have to stop and think before I give a response." "I feel silly saying things like that."

"Why say the child's words back to him?"

Reflective listening is not simply parroting the child's words. Rather, it is an indication that you are trying to understand the feeling and the meaning of the child's message.

Although children sometimes send feeling messages directly ("I hate that kid!"), usually the feeling is expressed by body language and tone of voice, rather than by words. For example: A child is crying and says, "All the kids pick on me!" The child's tone of voice and tears tell you of the hurt, yet the child did not say, "All the kids pick on me, and I feel hurt." A good listener is sensitive to the feeling that accompaniès the

message: "You're hurt when the kids pick on you." When you catch the feeling and reflect it, the child knows you understand.

When children send their feelings directly ("I hate that kid!") you can respond by simply acknowledging the feeling: "You are really angry with him!" Notice that that response was different from parroting. Parroting would be just bouncing back the child's words with no indication that you care or understand.

"I don't like to have to stop and think before giving a response."

If you are satisfied with your communication with your children, perhaps you have no need to learn reflective listening. With most parents, though, responding impulsively leads to miscommunication. Impulsive responses are likely to reinforce children's mistaken goals. Impulsive parents are easily manipulated by their children because they do exactly what the children expect.

"I feel silly saying things like that."

We can only say that any new behavior is uncomfortable. You have used your present pattern of responses for a long time; it is difficult to change. Learning new responses is like learning any other new skill. When one first tries the correct grip on a tennis racket or a golf club, it seems strange and unnatural. With practice, it feels familiar and almost natural. In the same way, as you become aware of how reflective listening improves the relationship between you and your child, it will begin to be natural.

How Children Respond When Parents First Begin Reflective Listening

Since reflective listening will be as new to the child as it is to you, expect a startled reaction to your first attempts. The child may look surprised and acknowledge your statement with, "Yeah, that's right," and walk away. At this point you could attempt to keep communication open with, "Would you like to tell me more about it?" Or, depending upon the situation, you could make no response and wait for another opportunity.

It is important not to try to force the child to share his or her feelings. This new experience may be embarrassing to the child, and your well-intentioned responses may be seen as attempts to invade the child's privacy. A power contest could result if you attempt to push the matter. There will be many opportunities to try again, if you make attempts to respond to the child's invitations. The child is free to accept or reject your offer of help. Don't be discouraged if the child does not respond quickly; remember this is a new experience which may be uncomfortable for the child.

Some children will want to continue talking with you about their feelings. This is especially true if they harbor intense feelings such as anger, hurt, or sadness. Your response may open the door for a dramatic exchange. For example, your child may charge, "You never let me do anything!" You respond with, "You're angry and feel I'm unfair." The child may come back with, "Yeah, you sure are! You treat me like a baby!" Now what do you do? Don't panic; keep reflecting: "It seems to you that I don't trust you." Then continue reflecting until it seems as if the problem is worked out or until the child's tone and behavior indicate a desire to stop.

Children don't always work through their problems in the listening sessions. Just as often, your patience and efforts to help them see the problems more clearly enable them to handle the problems on their own, outside the listening session.

Don't be concerned about doing reflective listening "just right." You don't have to do it perfectly. If you are sincere in an attempt to understand but mis-identify the feeling, the child will let you know, and you can try again.

Also, don't give up if reflective listening doesn't work right away. You can't expect it, or *any other* behavior change on your part, to work immediately. Your children have experienced you in familiar ways for quite some time. Your behavior has confirmed their goals. They may not be willing to change the behavior which has paid off for them just because you have decided to change. *It will take them time to realize that former behavior patterns no longer work for them.* Remember: Practice *plus* patience *equals* progress.

A Feeling Word List

Parents sometimes find it difficult to think of words to explain feelings. To help you, we have devised a list of "feeling words." See if you can add to it.

Words for Reflecting "Upset" Feelings

Note: Avoid overusing the word "upset." Frequently replying, "You're upset" may communicate that you do not understand. Be specific in your responses.

accused	hurt
angry	inadequate
anxious	incapable
bored	left out
defeated	miserable
difficult	put down
disappointed	rejected
discouraged	sad
disrespected	stupid
doubt	unfair
embarrassed	unhappy
feel like giving up	unloved
frightened	want to get even
guilty	worried
hate, hated	worthless
hopeless	

Words for Reflecting "Happy" Feelings

accepted	good
appreciated	grateful
better	great
capable	happy
comfortable	love
confident	pleased
encouraged	proud
enjoy	relieved
excited	respected
glad	satisfied

How to Construct a Reflective Listening Response

Parents sometimes find themselves blocked when they want to respond to the child's feelings and meanings. Reflective listening is a skill which requires effort and practice. You cannot expect to be a skilled listener when you are first learning.

We have found the following method helpful in learning how to listen reflectively:

When your child sends a feeling message, think to yourself: "What is she/he feeling?" Think of a feeling word that describes the emotion being expressed. For example, your son says: "I'll sure be glad when school's out! It's stupid." (Question: "What is he feeling?" Possible answer: bored.) Now put the feeling word into a sentence: "You seem to be saying you're bored with school."

If you concentrate on asking yourself the question, "What is my child feeling?" you will find your reflective listening response comes much easier.

Some Cautions about Using Reflective Listening

Keep your feedback statements tentative. You can't be sure you know exactly what the child is feeling. Watch your tone of voice and avoid sounding like a mind reader.

Reflective listening can be overdone. Constantly bombarding the child with reflective listening can cause her or him to avoid communication with you. Don't respond to every frown or comment. *Use discretion.* With sensitivity you can recognize when your child wants to talk and when he or she does not.

Reflective listening can sometimes reinforce a child's mistaken goal. For example, if your child continues to bring you the same or a similar problem time after time, it may be that she or he has discovered an effective way to get your attention or sympathy and has no intention of solving the problem. Unless you redirect this behavior, the child will learn to use problems to gain attention.

If your child is presently using problems merely to gain attention, an effective response could be, "We've discussed this problem several times before. I guess I can't help you with it; but I'm sure you'll be able to handle it." If the child persists, remain silent and busy yourself with other things, or change the subject. Although the child may be displeased with this response, the child will eventually learn that you are willing to help only if he or she will put forth an effort to solve the problem.

At times your child may be using his or her feelings to gain power over you or for revenge. Depending on the situation, you may decide to listen or withdraw from provocation.

At such times when you must displease a child by refraining from listening, be sure also to give positive attention; for example, by recognizing the child's contributions and spending some enjoyable time together.

Once you have gained skill in reflective listening, you are ready for the next step: exploring alternatives. Usually children can solve their own problems simply through being heard by a sympathetic adult; however, they can gain wider experience in problem solving when an adult helps them consider the advantages and disadvantages of various courses of action.

You will learn how to explore alternatives in Chapter 5.

QUESTIONS

1. What is suggested by the recommendation to treat our children as friends?

2. The authors mention seven traditional roles adults play when responding to children's feelings. Do you notice yourself playing any of these roles? Which ones?

3. What is involved in being a good listener?

4. What is reflective listening? In what sorts of situations would it be useful with your children?

5. What is meant by a "closed response"? Can you think of some examples of closed responses other than those given by the authors?

6. What is meant by an "open response"? Can you think of examples of open responses other than those given by the authors?

7. What is the difference between closed and open responses in terms of their effect on the child?

8. What do the authors mean by "listening" to behavior?

9. How can you influence children to discuss their feelings when their nonverbal behavior indicates that they are upset?

10. How is reflective listening different from parroting?

11. How is a reflective listening response constructed?

12. What are some of the cautions the authors mention about using reflective listening?

PROBLEM SITUATION

Tom's parents give him an allowance so that he can learn to budget his money. One day, Tom saw a new toy advertised on television and rushed in to tell his mother about it. He asked if he could buy the toy. Mother replied that it was up to him to decide what to do with his money. He complained that he did not have enough to buy the toy. Mother suggested that he save his allowance for a couple of weeks. Tom, though, didn't want to wait. He asked for a loan. Mother replied that loaning money was not her policy. Tom became angry and tried to provoke her into an argument.

1. What was Tom's goal?

2. What would be a parent's typical reaction?

3. If you decided to use reflective listening in a situation like this, what would you say?

4. Is there another response besides reflective listening which would be consistent with democratic child-rearing principles?

ACTIVITY FOR THE WEEK

Practice using reflective listening in your communication with your children.

CHART 4

Effective Listening

Closed Response
Denies children a right to their feelings by demonstrating listener's unwillingness to accept and understand.

Open Response
Acknowledges children's right to their feelings by demonstrating that the listener accepts what they feel as well as what they say. Indicates that the listener understands.

Child's Remark:	Closed Response:	Open Response:
I'm never going to play with her again!	Why don't you forget it; she probably didn't mean it.	You're really angry with her.
I can't do it!	Now, don't talk like that! You just got started!	It seems very difficult to you.
I wish I could go along. He always gets to go everywhere.	We've discussed this before — so, stop fussing.	It seems unfair to you.
Look at my new model!	That's nice . . . now will you please go . . .	You're pleased with your work on it.
I don't want to go to school today. Billy is mean!	Everyone has to go to school. It's the law.	You're afraid Billy will pick on you.
You're the meanest mother in the whole world!	Don't you *ever* talk to me that way!	You're very angry with me.

For each remark, give an example of a CLOSED response and an OPEN response.

1. I don't *like* vegetables, and I'm *not* going to eat them. _____

2. Our teacher is crabby. _____

3. I don't *want* to go to bed! It's too early. _____

4. I'm not going to wear my raincoat. Nobody in my class wears a stupid old raincoat. _____

POINTS TO REMEMBER

Communication: Listening

1. Communication begins by listening and indicating you hear the child's feelings and meanings.

2. Effective listening involves establishing eye contact and posture which clearly indicate you are listening.

3. Avoid nagging, criticizing, threatening, lecturing, probing, and ridiculing.

4. Treat your children the way you treat your best friend.

5. Mutual respect involves accepting the child's feelings.

6. Reflective listening involves hearing the child's feelings and meanings and stating this so the child feels understood.
It provides a mirror for the child to see himself or herself more clearly.

7. Learn to give open responses that accurately state what the other person feels and means.

8. Avoid closed responses which ignore the child's feelings, relaying that we have not heard or understood.

9. Let the child learn. Resist the impulse to impose your solutions.

My Plan for
Improving Relationships

(An opportunity to assess progress each week)

My specific concern:

My usual response:

- [ ] talking, lecturing
- [ ] noticing, nagging
- [ ] becoming angry

- [ ] punishing, removing privileges, shaming
- [ ] threatening, warning
- [ ] other_____

My progress this week:

	I am doing this more	I am doing this less	I am remaining about the same		I am doing this more	I am doing this less	I am remaining about the same
Listening	[ ]	[ ]	[ ]	Withdrawing from conflict	[ ]	[ ]	[ ]
Acting firmly and kindly	[ ]	[ ]	[ ]	Using consequences	[ ]	[ ]	[ ]
Becoming consistent	[ ]	[ ]	[ ]	Stimulating self-reliance	[ ]	[ ]	[ ]
Encouraging	[ ]	[ ]	[ ]	Stimulating responsible decision making	[ ]	[ ]	[ ]
Practicing mutual respect	[ ]	[ ]	[ ]				
Communicating love	[ ]	[ ]	[ ]	Taking time for fun	[ ]	[ ]	[ ]

I learned:

I plan to change my behavior by:

CHAPTER 5

Communication: Exploring Alternatives and Expressing Your Ideas and Feelings to Children

This reading will deal with three topics: (1) exploring alternatives, (2) problem ownership, and (3) I-messages.

Exploring Alternatives

In the last chapter you learned the skill of reflective listening: how to help children feel understood by making open responses to their communication of emotions. Through your reflective listening, children can clarify their feelings and consider a problem more rationally. Sometimes they can discover their own solutions simply by being heard by an understanding adult; they may discover a solution during the listening session or afterward.

There are other times when children need help in considering various courses of action. Sensitive adults can help them explore alternatives and choose solutions that make sense to them.

The process of exploring alternatives should not be confused with giving advice. Giving advice, such as "Do this . . . ." or, "I think you should . . . ." is not helpful, for the following reasons:

1. Advice does not help children learn to solve their own problems. It invites them to be dependent upon you.

2. Many children resist taking advice. They are either skeptical that your advice will work or they don't want to do what you say.

3. If your advice doesn't work, guess who is held responsible.

To help a child explore alternatives means to assist the child in identifying and considering the options available to solve a problem. It means to help the child evaluate each course of action and then to obtain a commitment to action.

The steps in exploring alternatives are:

1. USE REFLECTIVE LISTENING TO UNDERSTAND AND CLARIFY THE CHILD'S FEELINGS:

   "You're angry . . . ."
   "It seems to me that you feel . . . ."

2. EXPLORE ALTERNATIVES THROUGH BRAINSTORMING:

"Shall we look at some things you could do about this?"

"If you're interested in getting along better with your teacher, what are some things you could do?"

Get as many ideas from the child as possible.

3. ASSIST THE CHILD TO CHOOSE A SOLUTION:

Help the child evaluate the various possibilities.

"Which idea do you think is the best one?"

4. DISCUSS THE PROBABLE RESULTS OF THE DECISION:

"What do you think will happen if you do that?"

5. OBTAIN A COMMITMENT:

"What have you decided to do?"

"When are you going to do this?"

6. PLAN A TIME FOR EVALUATION:

"How long will you do this?"

"When shall we discuss this again?"

Be careful not to enter into exploring alternatives too soon. If you move too fast, the child may not be ready. Occasionally you may have to back up and limit yourself to reflecting the child's feelings until she or he is ready to move on to exploring alternatives.

There may be times when the child cannot generate plausible ideas, owing to lack of experience. In these instances, offer suggestions in a *tentative* form: "Have you considered what might happen if you . . . ?"

Keep suggestions to a minimum, so that the child is not invited to depend on you for ideas.

Again: Appropriate *timing* is essential. We recommend that you limit your responses to reflective listening until your child is expressing freely. Do not rush into the process of exploring alternatives; otherwise, your child may think you are being manipulative. There must be open communication for exploration of alternatives to be effective.

The Concept of Problem Ownership

The techniques of reflective listening and exploring alternatives are especially helpful when the child is the one experiencing the problem. There remains a question of what to do when *you* are the one experiencing a problem with your children. Before you examine the options open to you, consider the question of problem ownership. To determine problem ownership, simply ask, *whose problem is it?* Who is experiencing difficulty with whom? Whose purposes are not being met? Dr. Thomas Gordon* defines problem ownership in the following manner:

1. The child has a problem because he is thwarted in satisfying a need. It's not the parents' problem because the child's behavior in no way interferes with them. Therefore, the child owns the problem.

2. The child is satisfying his own needs — he is not thwarted — and his behavior is not interfering with the parents. Therefore, there is no problem in the relationship.

3. The child is satisfying his own needs — he is not thwarted. But his behavior is a problem to the parents because it is interfering with them. Now the parent owns the problem.

Once you determine who owns the problem, you are in a position to take action. If your child owns the problem, you may decide (depending upon the situation) to listen, to explore alternatives, or to allow the child to face the consequences independently. If you find that you are

*Gordon, Thomas, *Parent Effectiveness Training* (New York: Peter H. Wyden, Inc., 1970) p. 64.

the owner of the problem, several other courses of action may be open to you.

In this chapter we will discuss how to talk with children so that they will want to listen.

I-Messages

To influence your child, you must be able to communicate in a manner which makes it likely that your feelings, meanings, and intentions are being understood. In many families, parents do not expect children to listen; they expect to have to repeat every request at least once. Their children have trained them to repeat every message.

Parents sometimes create conditions which invite their children not to listen. For example: When we talk without expecting to be heard, we are training our children to be "parent-deaf." If our children are expected to take us seriously only when we "let them know we really mean it," we are training them to tune us out at other times.

When talking with your children, it is helpful to think in terms of "You-messages" and "I-messages."

The You-message lays blame and conveys criticism of the child. It suggests that the child is at fault. It is simply a verbal attack.

In contrast, an I-message simply describes how the child's behavior makes you feel. The message focuses on you, not on the child. It reports what you feel. It does not assign blame.

For example:

"When you wear your good clothes out to play, they wear out quickly, and I get con-

cerned because we can't afford to buy new ones."

I-messages express what the sender is feeling. They are specific. In an I-message, the nonverbal elements, such as tone of voice, are crucial. I-messages require a nonjudgmental attitude. An I-message delivered in anger becomes a You-message conveying hostility.

We are not trying to say that one should never be angry with one's children. The difficulties lie not in the anger itself, but in the purpose of the anger which may be to control, win, or get even. One should also be aware of the frequency of the use of anger. Frequent use of anger often produces the following results:

1. A child's goal of power or revenge is reinforced. When you get angry, the child knows that his/her attempts to provoke you have succeeded.

2. Communication is stifled. The child feels threatened and becomes defensive or counterattacks in an effort to save face.

If the relationship between parent and child is based on mutual respect, occasional anger can "clear the air" and foster communication. But if the relationship is not soundly based (i.e., if parent and child have frequent conflicts), the use of anger can do further damage. If your relationship with your own children is in the latter category, consider doing the following:

1. Become aware of the purpose(s) of your anger, and

2. Look for alternatives to using anger as a way to relate to your child.

Constructing an I-Message

Before expressing your feelings of displeasure to the child, consider this: It is usually not the child's behavior per se that's displeasing you; but, rather, the consequences the behavior produces for you — how it interferes with your needs or rights. If the child's behavior did not produce these consequences, you would probably not be bothered by it (unless it were harmful or dangerous). To illustrate: You are in the kitchen preparing dinner. Your children are busily playing in the other end of the house, laughing and having a good time. Their noise doesn't bother you. Then the phone rings. Now their behavior is interfering with your own needs; you feel displeased because you cannot hear what the other person is saying.

To repeat: Is it the children's behavior per se (their play) that is disturbing you, or is it the consequences their behavior has for you? Obviously, the disturbing element is the frustration — the consequences their behavior holds for you. Therefore, when you tell children how you feel about their behavior, let them know that your feelings relate to the *consequences* of their behavior, rather than to the behavior itself: "With all the noise, I'm having a difficult time hearing."

Because we want to focus on the consequences the behavior creates for us, rather than on the behavior itself, an I-message generally has three parts. It can be constructed by following these steps:

1. *Describe* the *behavior* which is interfering with you. (Just describe; don't blame.)
   "When you don't call or come home after school . . ."

2. State your *feeling* about the consequence the behavior produces for you.
   ". . . I worry that something might have happened to you . . ."

3. State the *consequence.*
   ". . . because I don't know where you are."

In summary, an I-message generally refers to three elements of a situation:

1. Behavior
2. Feeling
3. Consequence

A simple procedure, or formula, is helpful in constructing many I-messages. Think of stating an I-message by using the following phrases:

1. When you (state the *behavior*),
2. I feel (state the *feeling*),
3. because (state the *consequence*).

If we take the earlier example and put it in this formula, we have, *"When you* don't call or come home after school, *I* worry that something might have happened to you, *because* I don't know where you are." Stress the word *because* so the child will know that your feeling is related to the consequence, not the behavior itself.

The parts of an I-message do not have to be delivered in order; nor does an I-message always have to contain a statement of feeling. The example of the parent trying to talk on the phone was an I-message which described only the behavior and the consequences. Other examples are:

"I can't hear the television when there is so much noise."

"I can't cut the lawn when the toys are all over it."

Construction of an I-message depends upon the situation. The most important things to remember about I-messages are that they focus on *you*; they do not focus on the child; and they do not place blame on anyone.

Communicating to Children That We Value and Respect Them

The kind of communication we seek emerges from a relationship in which the child feels respected. It also depends on good timing. If you want to improve your relationship with your

child, find the proper time for a friendly talk. It's usually best not to try talking in the midst of conflict or dispute. At such times, it's best to withdraw from the conflict, maintaining mutual respect. Your display of respect during times of conflict makes it possible to open discussion at a later time.

Communication based on mutual respect also rests on your willingness to admit the limits of your knowledge; to admit that you do not have all the answers. If you cannot answer a child's question, don't try faking an answer. Instead, invite the child to seek it with you. Children are very sensitive to their parents' credibility, and feel embarrassed when their parents try to fake or bluff about knowledge they lack.

Sarcasm and ridicule not only stifle communication; they are destructive to human relationships. Children must be allowed to express their feelings without fear of being put down. When parents establish a climate free of fear, their children are able to reveal their feelings.

When we speak, we communicate our beliefs and values. If you believe your children are able, worthy, and well intentioned, you will communicate that through the words and gestures you use.

"Billy is usually stubborn." "Cindy can't do math." Unfortunately, children tend to make our labels come true. Labeling puts one into the role of judge — a counterproductive attitude in raising children. Faith in the child will help you avoid the use of labels. It is important to communicate your love and appreciation to your child.

To summarize: effective *communication* involves *both* listening and talking:

1. Purposeful conversation — talking with each other in order to understand what the other means.

2. Reflective listening responses which indicate you understand the child's feelings.

3. I-messages — blame-free messages about your positive feelings and about things that bother you.

4. A nonjudgmental attitude which respects the child.

5. Appropriate timing.

6. Restricting talk to friendly exchanges as much as possible.

7. Avoiding pressure, sarcasm, and ridicule.

8. Avoiding labeling.

9. Showing your faith and confidence in your child.

QUESTIONS

1. What is meant by "exploring alternatives"?

2. How does exploring alternatives differ from giving advice? Why is giving advice often ineffective?

3. What are the steps in exploring alternatives?

4. What can you do when your child is not able to generate ideas due to lack of experience?

5. When should you enter into exploring alternatives with your child?

6. What do the authors mean by "problem ownership"? Why is it important to recognize who owns the problem?

7. Why don't children listen to their parents?

8. What is an "I-message"? How is an "I-message" different from a "You-message"?

9. How is an "I-message" constructed? Why is it important to communicate to the child that the consequence of her or his behavior is what is disturbing you, rather than the behavior itself?

10. Why do parents use sarcasm and ridicule? What are the effects of these disciplinary methods on the child and on the parent?

11. How do your beliefs about your children affect your communication with them? How can you communicate your faith in your children?

EXERCISE 1

To determine problem ownership, consider the following:

1. If a child is hindered in satisfying a purpose, then *the child* owns the problem. The parents do not own the problem because the child's behavior does not interfere with them.

2. If the child is satisfying his or her own purposes and the child's behavior is not interfering with the parents, then there is no problem in the relationship.

3. If the child is satisfying his or her own purposes but the child's behavior is interfering with the parents, then *the parents* own the problem.

PROBLEM LIST: WHO OWNS THE PROBLEM?

Mark a "P" if the parent owns the problem and a "C" if the child owns it.

Who Owns the Problem?

1. Misbehavior in public when the parents are present . . . . ☐

2. Fighting with brothers and sisters . . ☐

3. Leaving belongings around the house . . . . ☐

4. Misbehavior at school . . . . ☐

5. Homework not done . . . . ☐

6. Not going to bed on time . . . . ☐

7. Uncooperative in morning routine . . ☐

8. Messing up the kitchen . . . . ☐

9. Misbehavior at the dinner table . . . . ☐

10. Not getting along with peers . . . . . . ☐

EXERCISE 2

I-messages generally have three parts, though not necessarily delivered in this order:

1. *Describe* the *behavior* which is interfering with you. (Just describe; don't blame.)

"When you don't call or come home after school . . ."

2. State your *feeling* about the consequence the behavior produces for you.

"...I worry that something might have happened to you..."

3. State the *consequence.*

"...because I don't know where you are."

PRACTICE SITUATIONS

Design an I-message for each situation:

1. Your son, who just got his driver's license, is backing out of the driveway too fast.

2. You are planning to have company. Your child promises to be home early and help prepare for guests. The child comes home late, causing you inconvenience.

3. You have just washed the car. Your child makes a design on it with muddy hand-prints.

4. Your child forgets to feed the dog.

5. Your child uses a paintbrush to paint a piece of wood and forgets to place the brush in turpentine.

PROBLEM SITUATION

Your daughter's teacher calls to complain about her behavior in school. The child is not complet-ing her assignments in class and does not seem at all interested in certain subjects. The teacher is angry and insists that you take corrective action. You believe the problem is between your daughter and the teacher. You also believe that your interference would prompt the girl to seek revenge on the teacher and cause problems in your parent-child relationship.

1. What might be the purpose of the teacher's behavior?

2. What faulty beliefs might you have which could interfere in your dealings with the teacher?

3. How can you apply what you have learned about communication skills to help you re-solve this problem with the teacher?

ACTIVITY FOR THE WEEK

Practice using I-messages and helping your child explore alternatives.

CHART 5

Decisions for Effective Communication

This chart illustrates situations in which the parent determines problem ownership
and then decides whether to listen reflectively or to send an I-message.

Situation	Who Owns Problem?	Reflective Listening	I-Message
Child weeping about "low" report card.	Child	You're feeling discouraged about your grades, and maybe worried about what I will think of you.	
Child not helping clean house as agreed upon.	Parent		When you don't keep agreements, I feel it's unfair because I have to do all the work.
Child unable to sleep the night before a test.	Child	You're pretty worried about that test, and not sure you'll do very well.	
Guests visiting; child interrupting parents and guests.	Parent		We can't talk with each other when you keep interrupting.
Child downcast after losing a race.	Child	You're pretty disappointed that you lost.	

Exploring Alternatives and Expressing Your Ideas and Feelings to Children

1. Help the child explore alternative solutions:

  a. Use reflective listening to understand and clarify the child's feelings.

  b. Explore alternatives through brainstorming.

  c. Assist the child in choosing a solution.

  d. Discuss the probable results of the decision.

  e. Obtain a commitment.

  f. Plan a time for evaluation.

2. Decide who owns the problem. Ask yourself, "Whose purposes or desires are not being met?"

3. Behavior is a problem for you *only* when the behavior interferes with you.

4. Communicate your feelings with "I-messages." I-messages tell children how their behavior interferes with you and how you feel about this interference. Report your feelings, without assigning blame.

5. Use I-messages to communicate your positive feelings as well as to communicate things which bother you.

6. I-messages delivered in anger become You-messages. You-messages blame children and convey criticism but omit the message that it is the child's responsibility to change. You-messages are sent in disrespectful tones.

7. When there is a conflict, limit your talking to perception of feelings and answering questions. As much as possible, restrict talking to friendly conversation in a calm atmosphere.

8. Sarcasm, ridicule, and pressure are destructive to good relationships.

9. Avoid using labels which show a lack of confidence in your child.

10. Communicate faith in your child through words, gestures, and tone of voice.

My Plan for Improving Relationships

(An opportunity to assess progress each week)

My specific concern:

My usual response:

- ☐ talking, lecturing
- ☐ noticing, nagging
- ☐ becoming angry
- ☐ punishing, removing privileges, shaming
- ☐ threatening, warning
- ☐ other_____

My progress this week:

	I am doing this more	I am doing this less	I am remaining about the same		I am doing this more	I am doing this less	I am remaining about the same
Listening	☐	☐	☐	Withdrawing from conflict	☐	☐	☐
Acting firmly and kindly	☐	☐	☐	Using consequences	☐	☐	☐
Becoming consistent	☐	☐	☐	Stimulating self-reliance	☐	☐	☐
Encouraging	☐	☐	☐	Stimulating responsible decision making	☐	☐	☐
Practicing mutual respect	☐	☐	☐				
Communicating love	☐	☐	☐	Taking time for fun	☐	☐	☐

I learned:

I plan to change my behavior by:

Developing the Courage to Be Imperfect*

You have now passed the halfway point in STEP. At this point you might be feeling guilty — as if there has been "something wrong" with the way you have been raising your children. A parent, too, needs to develop the courage to be imperfect. With the courage to be imperfect, a parent can focus on the present time, rather than worry about the past.

Take a few minutes to consider the following points:

1. Children should be encouraged, not expected, to pursue perfection.

2. When we try to be better or "more" than other people, we are demonstrating our concern with self-elevation and with our own prestige rather than our concern for other people.

3. Are you motivated primarily to help others, or to be superior to others?

4. It is better to have the desire to be useful than to have the desire for self-elevation. The latter is accompanied by constant fear of making mistakes.

5. Mistakes can be regarded as aids to learning. Mistakes are not failures.

6. Anticipating the danger of a mistake makes us more vulnerable to error.

7. Too many human relationships are mistake-centered and fault-finding.

8. Mistakes are unavoidable and, in most cases, less important than what the individual does after he or she has made a mistake.

9. Limit yourself to what you can do. Don't try to correct or change too many things.

10. Develop a sense of your own personal strength and worth.

11. Mutual respect begins by valuing oneself.

12. Discouragement, fierce competition, unrealistically high standards, and overambition characterize many ineffective, unhappy human beings. High ambition is directly related to the depth of one's feelings of inferiority.

13. Develop the courage to cope with the challenges of living.

---

*The concept of The Courage to Be Imperfect was originally developed by Dr. Rudolf Dreikurs, an internationally known psychiatrist.

CHAPTER 6

Natural and Logical Consequences: A Method of Discipline That Develops Responsibility

One way to discipline children is to reward them when they obey and punish them when they disobey.

The reward-and-punishment method, which is the disciplinary system in which most parents of today were raised, has certain disadvantages:

• It makes parents responsible for their children's behavior.

• It prevents children from learning to make their own decisions and, consequently, from adopting rules for effective behavior.

• It suggests that acceptable behavior is expected only in the presence of authority figures.

• It invites resistance by attempting to force children to conform.

There is an alternative to reward and punishment. It is called "natural and logical consequences."*

This method has certain advantages over reward and punishment:

First, it holds children, not their parents, responsible for the children's behavior.

_____

*The term "natural and logical consequences" is attributed to Rudolf Dreikurs. See Dreikurs, Rudolf, and Grey, Loren, *A Parent's Guide to Child Discipline* (New York: Hawthorne Books, Inc., 1970).

Second, it allows children to make their own decisions about what courses of action are appropriate.

Third, it permits children to learn from the (impersonal) natural or social order of events, rather than forcing them to comply with the wishes of other persons. The child who refuses to eat goes hungry. The child who insists on not wearing mittens gets cold hands. Those are two examples of natural consequences. In situations devoid of natural consequences, or in instances of danger to a child, logical consequences can be substituted.

Logical consequences permit a child to learn from the reality of the social order. That is, they acknowledge mutual rights and mutual respect. For the consequences to be effective, the child must see them as logically related to their misbehavior. In other words, the consequences must "fit" the behavior in a logical way.

There are several major differences between logical consequences and punishment:

1. *Punishment expresses the power of personal authority:*

   Father: "Jim, turn off that TV! Mom and I are trying to sleep!"

   In contrast, logical consequences express the reality of the social order. Logical consequences acknowledge mutual rights and mutual respect.

   Father: (TV is blaring) "Jim, I realize it's Saturday morning and you enjoy your cartoons, but Mom and I are trying to sleep. So, either turn the TV down or play outside. You decide which you'd rather do."

2. *Punishment is arbitrary or barely related to the logic of the situation:*

   Mother: (angrily) "Susan! I've told you a thousand times to keep your room straightened up! I can't vacuum the carpets with all that mess on the floor, so you can forget about going to the movie Saturday night."

   In contrast, a logical consequence is related to the misbehavior.

   Mother: "Susan, I'm going to vacuum the carpets today. I can't vacuum in your room if there are toys and clothes lying around on the floor. So I'll place them in bags and put them in the basement if you decide not to pick them up."

3. *Punishment is personalized and implies moral judgment:*

   Father: (angrily) "You took my hammer without permission! Don't you know that's like stealing? You know stealing is wrong! And now you've lost it! Your allowance is cut off until the hammer is paid for!"

   Logical consequences are impersonal; they imply no element of personal moral judgment.

   Hugh borrowed Dad's hammer without permission. He lost the hammer. Dad handled the situation by focusing on the impersonal fact that the hammer must be replaced:

   Father: "How will you replace the hammer, Hugh?"

4. *Punishment is concerned with past behavior.*

   Ralph made an agreement to be home at five o'clock, but did not arrive until six o'clock.

   Mother: (angrily) "Ralph! It's six o'clock. You're always late! How many times have we gone through this? You never seem to care. You can just stay home for a week, and you can just forget about that bike we talked about."

   Logical consequences are concerned with present and future behavior.

Mother: (the next time Ralph asks to go out) "I'm sorry, but you're not ready to take responsibility for coming home on time. We'll try again tomorrow."

5. *Punishment threatens the "offender" with disrespect or loss of love; it is a put-down.*

Mother has told Charles he could have the privilege of playing with the dog if he would take responsibility for feeding and watering the animal.

Mother: (moralistically) "You did not feed Champ, so you may not play with him today. Maybe this will teach you the value of being responsible for your pet."

When logical consequences are invoked, the parent's voice is friendly and implies good will.

Charles: "Mom, I'm going to play with Champ now."

Mother: (matter-of-factly) "No, Charles; you haven't taken time to give him his food and water today. We'll try again tomorrow."

6. *Punishment demands obedience.*

Susan and Shelly are disturbing the meal by kicking each other under the table.

Father: "You two knock it off right now or you'll go to bed without supper!"

Logical consequences permit choice.

Father: "You may settle down or leave the table until you're ready to join us."

In addition to the foregoing major differences between punishment and logical consequences, there are important subtle differences. Anger, warnings, threats, and reminders may turn a consequence into a punishment.

Some parents control verbal expression of hostility, yet continue to communicate it non-verbally. These parents "shout with their mouths shut." They tend to send hidden messages that imply the child has committed a crime and needs to be punished. Their punitive attitude interferes with the benefit to the child of experiencing the logical consequences of a poor decision.

The purpose of allowing natural consequences to occur and of designing logical consequences is to encourage children to make responsible decisions, not to force their submission. This mode of discipline permits a child to choose and then to be accountable for the decision, whether it turns out well or not. Most children, when permitted to make poor decisions, learn from the consequences.

To illustrate how hidden motives may spoil a logical consequence, consider the following example:

Mrs. Campbell's two children usually create a disturbance in the back seat of the car. She would shout at them to be quiet. Her scolding would result in a few minutes of silence, followed by more disturbance.

When Mrs. Campbell learned about logical consequences, this is what happened:

The next time the children misbehaved, she pulled to the side of the road and said, "I can't drive with all this noise. When you settle down, I'll go on." To herself she thought: "That will make them be quiet."

The children settled down and she pulled back into traffic. The children soon began to misbehave again. She pulled to the side of the road and waited, saying nothing. The children settled down again, and Mother started off once more.

During the rest of the trip, Mrs. Campbell had to pull to the side of the road several times. The next time she took the children in the car, the same thing happened — even worse. Finally she gave up. No more logical consequences for her!

She returned to her former method of discipline, yelling at the children.

Mother's action (stopping the car until order was restored) was in the form of a logical consequence. *But* her *hidden motive* of *power* turned her consequence into a punishment. She was much too personally involved. Nonverbally she let it be known that her purpose was to force submission. The children sensed her intentions. Had she simply decided what she was going to do and impersonally let the children decide how to respond, she probably would have been effective. She may have had to stop a few times on the first trip to allow the children to discover that she meant what she said, but on the second outing, one stop would probably have been sufficient.

Mother could have increased her effectiveness by sincerely taking the children's wishes into consideration. In advance of the trip she might have asked the children whether they wanted to go with her. If they had said no, perhaps she could have arranged for someone to watch them. When we are considerate of children's wishes, we find them more cooperative.

Timing is extremely important to make logical consequences work. Dealing with misbehavior at the moment it occurs can lead to difficulty in maintaining positive parent-child relations. Except in emergencies or when a child is creating a disturbance, it's best to delay action until you can approach the problem calmly.

Remaining matter-of-fact and nonpunishing is extremely important. This means separating the deed from the doer. If you can view misbehavior objectively, rather than regarding it as a personal affront, you will be much more effective. If you were trying to teach your child a new skill, such as an athletic or musical skill, you would probably be patient. You would expect and accept mistakes. If you can learn to approach any sort of mistake this way, you will find it easier to regard misbehavior as a learning experience rather than a violation of parental authority.

Basic Principles

Several principles guide the use of natural and logical consequences:

Understand the Child's Goals, Behavior, and Emotions.

Natural consequences are effective regardless of the goal. They result from letting the child experience the reality of nature; they require no arrangement by the parent.

Logical consequences result from letting the child experience the reality of the social world. They are generally most appropriate for attention-getting behavior, because conflicts with the attention-getter are less intense than conflicts with a child who seeks power or revenge. A child whose goal is power or revenge usually views logical consequences as arbitrary punishment. Before using logical consequences, parents of such a child must concentrate on improving the relationship through respect and encouragement. They must be willing to postpone action on some conflicts until the relationship is improved.

Be Both Firm and Kind.

Most parents are either firm *or* kind. Few are firm *and* kind at the same time. Your tone of voice indicates your desire to be kind, while your follow-through with appropriate action indicates your firmness.

Do not interpret firmness as strictness or harshness. Strictness deals with the child; firmness deals with our own behavior and feelings. Strictness is a term relating to control of the child; firmness is an attitude toward one's decisions.

An example of firmness: "I am willing to have Therese stay overnight at our house only if both of you are willing to go to bed by 10 o'clock," with appropriate follow-through if the children stay up later than the time agreed upon.

Don't Try to Be a "Good" Parent.

Refrain from overprotecting. Allow the child to experience the consequences of his or her own decisions. Avoid taking responsibilities which are logically the child's.

Become More Consistent in Your Actions.

Though no human being is totally consistent, through increasing your consistency you let children know what to expect, so that they can make their decisions accordingly.

Separate the Deed from the Doer.

Your tone of voice and nonverbal behavior must indicate that you respect the child even when her or his behavior is not socially acceptable. Failure to show respect for the child will turn your consequence into punishment.

For example, Mr. K was talking on the telephone. His two children were fighting and arguing, making it impossible for him to hear. He said, "You two either quiet down or leave the room! I'm trying to talk on the phone!" The chil-

dren became quiet, but soon resumed their disturbance. "All right, you heard me! You kids leave the room until I'm through talking!" he ordered.

Although Mr. K gave his children a choice, his action was not tied to logical consequences. He had not separated the deed from the doer, and so his attitude and tone of voice made the consequence a punishment. He had not based his action on respect for the children as persons, separate from their deeds.

Encourage Independence.

Your children will be better prepared for responsible, happy adulthood if you let them become independent. The more you can help them become self-reliant, the more competent they will feel. Avoid doing for children what they can do for themselves.

Avoid Pity.

Many parents "protect" their children from responsibilities because they feel sorry for them. Pity is a very damaging attitude. It tells the recipient that he or she is somehow defective —

that he or she can't handle problems. Parents who pity their children often do not realize that overprotection handicaps children. Overprotection may serve to make an insecure parent feel stronger, but it does so at the child's expense.

Pity is not the same as empathy. Because we love our children, we want to show them we empathize, or understand, their feelings. Empathy promotes strength, whereas pity promotes weakness.

Refuse to Become Overconcerned about What Other People Think.

Many parents hesitate to allow children to accept the consequences of their behavior because they fear disapproval from their own parents or from parents-in-law, friends, neighbors, or teachers. Intimidated parents can gain courage from the realization that children are independent beings who must learn to decide how they will behave, and that children's behavior does not necessarily reflect on the parents as persons. Although other people may try to hold you accountable for everything your child does, their demands are not realistic. Parents cannot possibly be responsible for all their child's behavior.

Recognize Who Owns the Problem.

Parents assume ownership of many problems which are actually their children's. To extricate yourself from a dilemma, define the problem, decide whose it is, and act accordingly.

Talk Less, Act More.

Parents hinder their effectiveness by talking too much. A child easily becomes "parent deaf." Do most of your talking with children when you are on friendly terms and they are therefore willing to listen. When using logical consequences, keep talk to a minimum as you follow through with action.

Refuse to Fight or Give In.

Set limits and allow the child to decide how to respond to them. Be willing to accept the child's decision. You do not have to win, because you are not in a contest. Your goal is to help the child become responsible for his or her own behavior.

Example: On Friday, nine-year-old Cliff was invited to a Saturday matinee. He was to be at his friend's house for a ride at one o'clock. Cliff's mother told him that he could go *if* his chores were finished first. Cliff agreed; but he wasted away most of Saturday morning. His chores were not finished by the time to leave. When Cliff came to Mother for money for the movie, she

said, "I'm sorry, Cliff, but your chores are not done, so you'll have to miss the movie."

"Aww, Mom!" begged Cliff. "Can't I do them when I get home?"

"No, our agreement was that they would be finished before you went," answered Mother.

"Oh, *please,* Mom!" cried Cliff. "I've been waiting a long time to see this movie. *Please* let me go."

At this point Mother left the room, so that Cliff could not engage her in an argument. She then called the other parent to inform him that Cliff would not be going.

Wisely, Mother did not fight or give in. She had let Cliff decide how to respond to the limits. When he did not do his chores, Mother assumed he had decided not to go to the movie, since the agreement had been that the chores would be done before he went. Kindly and firmly, she followed through with the logical consequences of his decision.

Let All the Children Share Responsibility.

When an incident occurs in a group of children, don't try to find the guilty party. Fault-finding only increases rivalry among children. Let all share the responsibility. Have the children decide how to handle the problem. Do not listen to tattling.

For example: Mr. Jones constantly found candy wrappers, empty potato chip bags, dirty glasses, and so on, in the family room after the children finished watching TV. He told the children that if they wanted to snack in the family room, they would have to clean up after themselves.

The following evening, he found all the mess cleaned up, except for one dirty glass and a popcorn bowl. Father did not play detective. Instead, he decided not to allow any of the children to snack in the family room the next day. He believed all should share the responsibility and decide among themselves how they would regain the privilege of snacking in the family room.

Steps in Applying Consequences

1. *Provide choices.*

   Choice is essential in the use of logical consequences. Alternatives are proposed by the parent and the parent accepts the child's decision. Then the child makes a choice without external pressure.

   The parent's tone of voice is crucial. It must reflect an attitude of *respect, accept-*

ance, and *good will.* The choice of words is also important.

Examples of choices phrased in a respectful manner:

"Michelle, we're trying to watch TV. You may settle down and watch the program with us or leave the room. You decide which you'd rather do."

"If you plan to go outside after school, you'll need to change your clothes." The choice is obvious. (To state the alternate choice would be unnecessary.)

Some logical consequences involve stating your intentions and letting the child decide how to respond:

"Since you know how to get yourself ready for school, starting tomorrow morning you can be responsible for these things. Here's an alarm clock, and here is how you set it." (In this way Mother communicates that she is no longer willing to be responsible for the morning routine.)

"I'm willing to wash only what is in the hamper."

2. *As you follow through with a consequence, give assurance that there will be an opportunity to change the decision later.*

   After you give children a choice, they often decide to test the limits. When this happens, tell them that the decision stands, but that they may try again later.

   Mother: (following through matter-of-factly) "I see you have decided to leave the room. Feel free to come back when you are ready to settle down."

   Father: (following through matter-of-factly) "I see you haven't changed your clothes, so I assume you have decided to stay in today and try again tomorrow."

3. *If the misbehavior is repeated, extend the time that must elapse before the child may try again.*

   If children continue to misbehave, they are saying they aren't ready to be responsible.

   "I see that you're still not ready to settle down and have decided to leave the room. You may try again tomorrow night."

"I see by your clothes that you are choosing to stay in today. You may choose again in two days."

From this point on, the parent should *use no words* except to assure the child that she or he will have another opportunity to try again and to state the time (which should be increased again) at which the child will have another opportunity.

TV Situation: The parent should simply remove the child, saying, "You may try again the day after tomorrow."

Clothes-Changing Situation: "You may decide again in three days."

If you have difficulty applying consequences, check the steps involved to see if you clearly understand the principles. To make sure your action is not punishment, but an expression of logical consequences,

1. Show an "open" attitude: give the child a choice and accept the child's decision.

2. Use a friendly tone of voice which expresses good will.

3. Make sure the consequence is logically related to the misbehavior.

Following are some examples of the use of consequences for some typical daily difficulties.

Problem

Morning routine — getting up, getting dressed, eating breakfast, leaving for school.

Typical Reactions:

Take responsibility for child's morning routine — call several times, dress child, remind, coax, assist, nag, threaten, force, shove out door.

Natural and Logical Consequences:

Give child alarm clock and show him or her how to set it. Say that you expect child to be responsible for getting up, dressed, fed, and out the door.

The child, a parent, or someone else can prepare breakfast; but the child is the one who decides whether the child eats. If the child misses breakfast, *permit the natural consequences* of hunger to bring about a decision to allow time for breakfast after this.

If the child is late to school, let him or her experience consequences from the teacher. (Ahead of time, call the school to explain your actions and request their cooperation.)

If a child who takes the bus misses it because he or she has dawdled, the logical consequence would be that the child walk to school. (Do not drive the child to school. This would be a special service, and the child may decide that being taken to school by car is better than going by bus.) If there are dangerous corners or other hazards to prevent the child from walking, two choices are available to the parent:

1. *Change the morning routine.* If the child likes breakfast and would not like to miss it, announce that if anyone wishes to have time for

breakfast, she or he will need to be dressed and ready to leave before coming to the table. If the child dawdles and time runs short, announce that there is no time left for breakfast today. Add that there will be another opportunity for breakfast tomorrow.

2. *Allow the child to stay home, given certain conditions.* Establish a policy that the child may stay home from school for one reason only: sickness. If the child decides to stay home, you may assume she or he is not feeling well. The child will need to stay in bed until the next morning. The child may not play when other children come home from school, because he or she is "sick."

If you expect the child to involve you in a power struggle over staying in bed, you will need to change the approach. Allow the child to stay home, but act as if he or she is in school. Do not have any interaction with the child until the time he or she would normally come home from school. At noon the child will have to make his or her own lunch, for the child is not at home to you. You may wish to go on short shopping trips or to visit neighbors if the child is old enough to be left home alone.

Explanation

If you assume responsibility for your child's morning routine, the child will not learn to take this responsibility, but will expect others to. Not all children require a full breakfast, so let children learn from experience what is best for them. Children soon become tired of staying home "sick" or "alone."

Problem
Late for meals.

Typical Reactions:
Call several times, lecture, feed them after everyone else has finished, or send them to bed without supper.

Natural and Logical Consequences:
Allow children to be responsible for getting themselves to meals. Tell them that meals will be served at specific times. Say that you will call them once and that it's up to them to decide whether or not to come. If they are going to be away from home, inform them what time the meal will be served and let them be responsible for checking the time. If the meal is still being served when the children arrive, they may eat. (The consequence would be eating cold food.) If they miss the meal, they should go without food until the next meal, so that they will experience the natural consequences of hunger. The choice of whether or not to come to a meal on time — or to come at all — remains theirs.

Explanation
Continuing to call children several times, or searching for them when they don't show up, is giving them undue service. Lecturing or arbitrarily sending them to bed undermines the parent-child relationship. Heating their food or serving them after the rest of the family has finished also provides undue service and fails to teach them to be responsible for their own behavior.

Problem
Refusing to eat certain foods.

Typical Reactions:
Remind, coax, require children to eat a little of everything, fix special foods, prepare food on demand, use dessert as a reward.

Natural and Logical Consequences:
Prepare and place foods on the table. Do not fill the children's plates for them. Allow the children to decide whether or not to eat. They may eat whatever they wish of the foods offered, as long

as they do not deprive other family members of equal portions. The children should understand that no food will be served until the next meal.

In any problem involving eating, remove as many snacks as possible so as not to get into battles with children who might try to sneak snacks.

Explanation

Eating is a bodily function and should not become a subject for battle. Forcing children to eat certain foods creates resentment and increases their dislike of the foods. Adults readily admit to not eating some things; the principle of mutual respect suggests that children should not be expected to eat every food, either.

Preparing special foods for children only gives them the impression they are entitled to special consideration. However, children's preferences should be considered. At family meetings, children can help plan the week's menu. For variety, at some meals the family may eat what the children like. Other meals will consist of what the parents prefer. Or each family member could plan a meal around the foods he or she chooses. Family members could then decide who would prepare this meal for the family.

Using dessert as a reward only increases the children's resentment and teaches them to trade behavior for desired payoffs. If dessert is part of the meal, it should be offered to everyone.

Problem
Coming to the table dirty.

Typical Reactions:
Lecture, send away from table to wash.

Natural and Logical Consequences:
Tell children that if they wish to come to the table, they will need to be clean. If they arrive dirty, simply remove their plates and say, "I see you are not ready to eat." Say no more. Do not return the plates until the children are clean. If they are not clean by the conclusion of the meal, assume they have decided to skip the meal and tell them they may try again at the next meal. Prevent snacking before the next meal.

Explanation
Coming to the table clean is the children's responsibility. You act with firmness by calmly removing their plates and allowing them to decide whether they intend to eat.

A Final Note about Logical Consequences
The line between punishment and logical consequences is thin at times. Your matter-of-fact tone of voice, friendly attitude, and willingness to accept the child's decision are essential characteristics of logical consequences.

No matter how logical an action may seem to you, if your tone is harsh, your attitude overbearing, and your demands absolute, your action is punitive.

It is important to recognize that consequences take time to be effective. When you are using consequences, you are changing from your typical responses. Your children may test the limits. Remember, patience *plus* practice *equals* progress.

QUESTIONS

1. Why do the authors suggest doing away with reward and punishment as a way to relate to children?

2. What alternatives to reward and punishment do the authors suggest?

3. Why are natural and logical consequences more effective than reward and punishment?

4. What is the difference between a natural consequence and a logical consequence?

5. The authors give the following examples of natural consequences:
   a. The child who refuses to eat goes hungry.
   b. The child who does not wear mittens has cold hands.

   Can you think of a challenge with your own children for which natural consequences would apply?

6. When should logical consequences be used instead of natural consequences?

7. How do logical consequences differ from punishment?

8. How can consequences be turned into punishment?

9. Why is it important to understand the child's goal and feelings before applying consequences?

10. What is meant by being *both* firm and kind?

11. Why is consistency important?

12. What is meant by "separating the deed from the doer"? Why is this principle important when using consequences?

13. Why is the principle "talk less, act more" important to remember?

14. What is meant by refusing either to fight or to give in?

15. Why is timing important in applying consequences?

16. Why is it important to let all the children involved in a problem share the responsibility?

17. What are the steps involved in applying consequences?

18. Can you think of a challenge with your child where logical consequences would apply?

EXERCISE

Below are examples of typical parent-child concerns. For each situation, do the following:

1. Identify an appropriate natural or logical consequence.
2. Label your consequences as natural or logical.
3. Decide how you would present the choice.
4. Decide what you would do or say after the child has chosen what he or she will do.

NOTE: In each situation, look for a natural consequence *first.* If a natural consequence is not available or is inappropriate, design a logical consequence. Make certain your action is truly a *logical* consequence, rather than a personal or arbitrary punishment. (You may wish to refer to Chart 6 or the list of major differences between punishment and logical consequences at the beginning of this chapter.)

PRACTICE SITUATIONS

1. Mr. and Mrs. Thompson's children leave their possessions strewn around the house. Both parents find themselves frequently yelling at the children or picking up after them. How can the Thompsons use consequences to handle this situation?

2. Every night at bedtime, Janet tries to get her parents' attention by asking for a drink of water, to go to the bathroom, etc. What can Janet's parents do?

3. Barbara, age eight, eats with her fingers. During each meal, her parents remind her several times to use the silverware provided. Still, Barbara continues to use her fingers. How can the parents help Barbara learn table manners?

4. Joey, age ten, and Ronnie, age seven, are constantly arguing. Usually their arguments develop into fights. When that happens, Ronnie runs to Mom or Dad howling that Joey hit him. The parents have tried everything to stop these fights. They have spanked Joey for hitting his younger brother; they have punished both for fighting; and they have found out which boy started the fight and punished him. The boys continue to argue and fight despite these actions by their parents. What can Mom and Dad do?

PROBLEM SITUATION

Mr. and Mrs. Jackson and their children, Susie and Jerry, are eating dinner in a restaurant. Jerry begins to create a disturbance by belching and giggling.

1. As a parent in a similar situation, what would be your probable feelings and likely reaction?
2. What alternatives are available to Mr. and Mrs. Jackson?
3. What is an appropriate logical consequence they might use?

ACTIVITY FOR THE WEEK

Practice applying natural or logical consequences to one of your child-training problems. Choose a situation in which you believe you can be successful.

CHART 6

The Major Differences between Punishment and Logical Consequences

PUNISHMENT

Character-istics	Underlying Message to Child	Likely Results
1. Emphasis on power of personal authority.	"Do what I say because I say so."	Rebellion. Desire for revenge. Lack of self-discipline. Sneakiness. Irresponsibility.
2. Rarely related to act; arbitrary.	"I'll show you." "You deserve what you're getting!"	Resentment. Desire for revenge. Fear. Confusion. Rebellion.
3. Implies moral judgment.	"You're bad! You're not acceptable."	Feelings of hurt, guilt. Desire to get even.
4. Emphasis on past behavior.	"You'll never learn. I can never count on you."	Feels unacceptable. Feels can't make good decisions.
5. Threats of disrespect, violence, or loss of love, either open or concealed.	"You'd better shape up!" "No child of mine would do a thing like that!"	Fear. Rebellion. Guilt feelings. Desire to "get back."
6. Demands compliance.	"Your preferences don't matter." "You can't be trusted to make wise decisions."	Rebellion. "Defiant compliance."

LOGICAL CONSEQUENCES

Character-istics	Underlying Message to Child	Likely Results
1. Emphasis on reality of the social order.	"I trust you to learn to respect the rights of others."	Cooperation. Respect for self and others. Self-discipline. Reliability.
2. Logically related to the misbehavior; sensible.	"I trust you to make responsible choices."	Learning from experience.
3. Treats person with dignity; separates deed from doer.	"You are a worthwhile person."	Senses he or she is acceptable even though behavior is not.
4. Concerned with present and future behavior.	"You are able to take care of yourself."	Becomes self-evaluating, self-directing.
5. Voice communicates respect and good will.	"I don't like what you are doing, but I still love you."	Feels secure about parent's love and support.
6. Presents choice.	"You are capable of deciding."	Responsible decisions. Increased resourcefulness.

Principles of Natural and Logical Consequences

1. Reward and punishment deny children the opportunity to make their own decisions and to be responsible for their own behavior.

2. Natural and logical consequences require children to be responsible for their own behavior.

3. Natural consequences are those which permit children to learn from the natural order of the physical world — for example, that not eating is followed by hunger.

4. Logical consequences are those which permit children to learn from the reality of the social order — for example, children who do not get up on time may be late to school and have to make up work.

5. For consequences to be effective, the children involved must see them as logical.

6. The purpose of using natural and logical consequences is to motivate children to make responsible decisions, not to force their submission. Consequences are effective only if you avoid having hidden motives of winning and controlling.

7. Be both firm and kind. Firmness refers to your follow-through behavior. Kindness refers to the manner in which you present the choice.

8. Talk less; act more.

9. When you do things for children that they can do for themselves, you are robbing them of self-respect and responsibility.

10. Differences between punishment and logical consequences:

a. Punishment expresses the power of personal authority. Logical consequences express the impersonal reality of the social order.

b. Punishment is rarely related to misbehavior. Logical consequences are logically related to misbehavior.

c. Punishment tells the child he or she is bad. Logical consequences imply no element of moral judgment.

d. Punishment focuses on what is past. Logical consequences are concerned with present and future behavior.

e. Punishment is associated with a threat, either open or concealed. Logical consequences are based on good will, not on retaliation.

f. Punishment demands obedience. Logical consequences permit choice.

11. Avoid fights; they indicate lack of respect for the other person. Do not give in; that indicates lack of respect for yourself.

12. Steps in applying logical consequences:

a. Provide choices and accept the child's decision. Use a friendly tone of voice that communicates your good will.

b. As you follow through with a consequence, assure children that they may try again later.

c. If the misbehavior is repeated, extend the time that must elapse before the child tries again.

13. Be patient, it will take time for natural and logical consequences to be effective.

My Plan for Improving Relationships

(An opportunity to assess progress each week)

My specific concern:

My usual response:

☐ talking, lecturing ☐ punishing, removing privileges, shaming

☐ noticing, nagging ☐ threatening, warning

☐ becoming angry ☐ other_____

My progress this week:

	I am doing this more	I am doing this less	I am remaining about the same		I am doing this more	I am doing this less	I am remaining about the same
Listening	☐	☐	☐	Withdrawing from conflict . .	☐	☐	☐
Acting firmly and kindly	☐	☐	☐	Using consequences	☐	☐	☐
Becoming consistent	☐	☐	☐	Stimulating self-reliance . . .	☐	☐	☐
Encouraging	☐	☐	☐	Stimulating responsible decision making	☐	☐	☐
Practicing mutual respect . .	☐	☐	☐				
Communicating love	☐	☐	☐	Taking time for fun	☐	☐	☐

I learned:

I plan to change my behavior by:

CHAPTER 7

Applying Natural and Logical Consequences to Other Concerns

In the last chapter, we presented the principles of natural and logical consequences. The lesson explained the concept of consequences and gave suggestions for meeting challenges posed by children during a typical day.

Following is an outline which deals with other challenges encountered by most parents. Be sure to use Chart 6 as a reference for identifying and applying consequences for each of these challenges.

Challenge: Forgetting

Typical Reactions:

Remind, coax, nag, threaten, punish, excuse.

Natural and Logical Consequences:

The consequence depends, of course, on who is affected by the children's forgetting. If children forget things which do not involve you, do not interfere. Let them experience any consequences which may result. For example: They may forget to take books, lunch money, or other items to school. The consequences would occur in school; therefore, the problem would not be yours.

If their forgetting interferes with your rights, you own the problem. The consequences you design will depend upon the situation. (NOTE: Check other challenges listed here to determine a consequence which fits the child's forgetting.)

Explanation

As a rule, parents should not interfere in the relationships between their children and other people. Noninterference is made easier by recognizing who owns the problems and by allowing children to learn from their own decisions.

Constant reminders interfere with children's learning to be accountable for their own behavior. Children are prevented from growing up — from becoming independent — when their parents constantly remind them of what they should do for themselves.

Challenge:
Clothing and Hairstyle

Typical Reactions:

Select and lay out children's clothes; try to control length and style of hair, when to comb it, etc.

Natural and
Logical Consequences:

If you are the one who buys the child's clothes, allow the child to help select them. If you are concerned about the suitability of clothing (e.g., fabric, matching), give choices within a range of selection at purchase time. Allow the child to have a choice about the clothes worn to school. At a relaxed time, show the child preferred matches and clothing suitable to the weather, if necessary. If the child insists on improper matches or out-of-season clothing, do not argue. If the child chooses to wear clothes that do not match, peers will let him or her know what is unacceptable. If the child chooses clothes inappropriate to the weather, allow him or her to experience the natural consequences of discomfort. (Exception may be taken in cold or severe weather which would cause serious chilling or could be dangerous.)

Older children can be given a clothing allowance and should be permitted, within their budgets, to make their own selection of clothes.

With their children's clothing parents have rights, too. If you and your children are going out in public, you have the right to specify the type of clothing they may wear. You can give them choices from their wardrobe appropriate to the occasion. If you think your children will try to involve you in a power contest about the choices you present, arrange in advance for a babysitter to be on call. Specify to the children the conditions of dress, the availability of a sitter,

and the time you will be leaving. If they are not ready by that time, assume they have decided to stay home, and call the sitter. At that point the children may try to hurry so they can go. Inform them that it is too late; that they indicated their decision by their behavior prior to departure time. Add that they may have an opportunity to try again next time.

Concerning hairstyle and grooming: These are minor areas, compared with other challenges parents encounter. We recommend that children choose their own hairstyles and how and when to groom their hair.

If you are taking a child out in public, you have the right to set the conditions of grooming.

Explanation

Each generation of children and teenagers has its own clothing and grooming fads. Allowing children the freedom to choose their clothes and hairstyles helps demonstrate acceptance and respect for their tastes. Thus it helps improve parent-child relationships. Battling over minor problems makes it more difficult to deal with major concerns.

Challenge:
Cleanliness

Typical Reactions:

Lecture, remind, shame, command.

Natural and
Logical Consequences:

Brushing teeth: Because bad breath is offensive, and especially because sweets and other snack items contain sugar and starch which can be harmful to teeth, you can give children the choice of brushing their teeth or giving up snacks until they are willing to assume the responsibility for brushing.

Bathing: Two logical consequences are available. You can tell children that wearing clean clothes on dirty bodies is not acceptable. Then it is up to them to decide whether to wear clean or dirty clothes. If they choose the latter, their peers will notice the odor and mention it. You can also tell children that you accept their right not to bathe, but that you have a right not to have to breathe body odor. If they choose not to bathe, you can give them a choice of leaving your presence or bathing.

Explanation

The habit of cleanliness is not developed through the parents' taking responsibility for it. Children will learn the value of cleanliness when they experience the logical consequences of remaining unclean.

Challenge:
Kitchen Chores

Typical Reactions:

Remind, coax, threaten, show anger, do job for child.

Natural and
Logical Consequences:

Setting and clearing the table, washing dishes, and emptying trash are chores which permit children an opportunity to contribute to the family. They should be discussed and established at family meetings (to be described in Chapter 8). An effective consequence for any unfinished kitchen chore is to delay the meal until the chore is completed. For example, if the table is not set, the meal cannot be served until the chore is done; the meal cannot be prepared if the kitchen is left messy because it is inconvenient and unpleasant to work in a messy kitchen.

State your intentions to the children and follow through: If the chores are not finished, meals cannot be prepared, and neither can snacks. If the children do not respond or if the situation occurs again, you and your spouse may decide to eat out and let the children decide what they will do. Don't be concerned about which children did not perform their chores. Let them all share responsibility for making it possible to prepare meals.

If the children are too young to be left alone and you cannot get anyone to watch them, bring in some food for yourself after the children have gone to bed.

Explanation

The family cannot function without everyone's help. Parents respect the children's rights by not nagging. They also respect their own rights, by refraining from performing the children's chores and by taking care of their own needs (by eating out or getting carry-outs).

To be concerned about which children did not do their jobs promotes competition; it implies that someone is "bad." Take for granted that the siblings are responsible for each other and will maintain discipline among themselves.

Challenge:
Non-Kitchen Chores

Typical Reactions:

Remind, coax, threaten, do job, deduct from allowance.

**Natural and
Logical Consequences:**

For wastebaskets located outside the kitchen, and for garbage cans which need to be taken to the curb and returned, an effective way to get the job done is to negotiate a service charge. Explain to your children that if you did not wish to do one of your jobs, such as washing the car, you would hire someone else to do it. Mention that you will do their jobs, but that you expect to be paid, since they are not your responsibility. Then negotiate a fee. Establish the job deadline. Tell the children that if the tasks are not done by that time, you will assume they have decided to hire your services. Do the jobs and present the bill at the next family meeting.

Explanation

Deducting from children's allowances mistakenly implies that they are being paid for their contributions. On the other hand, a service charge is a fee children negotiate to pay their parents to do a job that they are unwilling to perform. We do not believe in paying children to do necessary chores around the house. After all, no one pays Mother or Father to. Children have a right to share in the family income and a related obligation to share in the upkeep of the home.

Chores in many families are dictated by the parents. Children resent having no choice in deciding what they will do. When the family makes up a list of chores together at a family meeting and all members choose their jobs, children are more willing to cooperate. Participation in decision making gives children a sense of their own worth. The family can decide together what to do about chores no one chooses. (In Chapter 8, you will learn more about conducting family meetings.)

QUESTIONS

1. What are logical consequences? How are logical consequences different from punishment?

2. The authors present natural and logical consequences for typical challenges presented by children. As an example, let's talk about the child who frequently seems to forget things:

   a. How do we usually react?

   b. What would be an appropriate logical consequence, and why would it be more effective than the typical reactions are?

EXERCISE 1

For each situation, decide how you can act instead of react.

1. While having lunch at the kitchen table, your son accidentally spills milk.

2. In a department store, your daughter begs for a toy. You feel she has enough toys.

3. You are trying to talk with your spouse. Your son keeps interrupting.

4. You have told your daughter not to leave her bicycle in the driveway. She continues to leave it there anyway.

EXERCISE 2

Do the following for each practice situation:

1. Decide who owns the problem.

2. Decide which of the three approaches to use:
   Approach 1: Reflective listening and exploring alternatives.
   Approach 2: I-messages.
   Approach 3: Natural or logical consequences.

3. Decide exactly what you would do or say.

PRACTICE SITUATIONS

1. You are trying to read. Your children are playing in another room. They become very noisy.

2. Your daughter expresses a desire to take guitar lessons. She is enthusiastic at first, but later begins to lose interest in practicing. You are concerned because you are paying for weekly lessons.

3. Your boy comes home crying. He complains that a neighbor child has hit him.

4. You and your spouse leave for work before your ten-year-old leaves for school, and the child returns home before you do. You have given the child a key for locking up and entering the house. You come home early one day and find the house unlocked.

PROBLEM SITUATION

The O'Neils are visiting friends. Five-year-old Billy begins misbehaving at the dinner table. Mrs. O'Neil, who has studied democratic child-training procedures, disregards those principles and sternly reprimands Billy. The child stops for a few moments, but begins again. After further embarrassment, Mrs. O'Neil excuses herself, takes Billy to another room, and closes the door. She returns to the table and apologizes to the hosts, who try to reassure her.

1. How do you feel about what happened?

2. Why might Mother have violated the child-rearing principles?

3. Why was she embarrassed?

4. What other alternatives consistent with democratic principles were available?

ACTIVITY FOR THE WEEK

Choose one of your own child-training challenges, in which you have unintentionally reinforced the child's misbehavior by doing what the child expects. Use the principle of "Acting — Not Reacting" to plan an effective response.

CHART 7

Selecting the Appropriate Approach

Problem	Who Owns Problem?	Appropriate Approach
Child borrows father's tools and does not return them.	**Parent**	**I-Message** — "When you don't return my tools, I get upset because I need them." or **Logical Consequence** — Deny child loan of tool next time he or she wants to borrow it.
Child is upset about failing test.	**Child**	**Reflective Listening** — "You're very sad about failing the test." **Exploring Alternatives** — "What are some things you can do next time you have a test?"
Child neglects homework.	**Child**	**Logical Consequence** — Allow child to face consequences from teacher.
Crawler touches light socket.	**Parent**	**Logical Consequence** — Place child in play-pen for short while. Then let child out. If child approaches socket again, place in pen for longer period.

For each of the following, decide who owns the problem and determine an appropriate approach:

1. Child does not lock up his or her bicycle. _____

2. Child does not return milk carton to refrigerator. _____

3. Infant in high chair throws food. _____

POINTS TO REMEMBER

Applying Natural and Logical Consequences; Acting— Not Reacting; and Selecting the Appropriate Approach

1. Parents' typical reactions often reinforce the children's goals of attention, power, revenge, or display of inadequacy. To remedy this, do the unexpected; practice the principle of "Acting — Not Reacting."

2. When using natural or logical consequences, remember to remain calm, show good will, give choices, and be willing to accept the child's decision.

3. Three effective approaches to problems in parent-child relations are:

   a. Reflective listening and exploring alternatives.

   b. I-messages.

   c. Natural and logical consequences.

4. The approach you select will primarily depend upon who owns the problem.

5. Your choice of approach will also depend upon your estimate of the effectiveness of each approach with your own children.

6. Children will sometimes use and repeat problems to gain your attention or sympathy. If this occurs, discontinue reflective listening and exploring alternatives.

7. Overuse of I-messages may cause children to become tired of hearing about your feelings. They may stop listening or "trap" you into using I-messages to give them attention or to engage you in a power struggle.

8. Some things children do should be ignored. Ignoring is a form of a logical consequence.

9. As mutual respect is established and the relationship improves, you may not have to use consequences as frequently.

10. Encouragement is implicit in all three approaches. Each approach expresses acceptance of the child, faith in his or her ability to solve problems, and respect for the child.

My Plan for Improving Relationships

(An opportunity to assess progress each week)

My specific concern:

My usual response:

☐ talking, lecturing   ☐ punishing, removing privileges, shaming

☐ noticing, nagging   ☐ threatening, warning

☐ becoming angry   ☐ other_____

My progress this week:

	I am doing this more	I am doing this less	I am remaining about the same		I am doing this more	I am doing this less	I am remaining about the same
Listening	☐	☐	☐	Withdrawing from conflict	☐	☐	☐
Acting firmly and kindly	☐	☐	☐	Using consequences	☐	☐	☐
Becoming consistent	☐	☐	☐	Stimulating self-reliance	☐	☐	☐
Encouraging	☐	☐	☐	Stimulating responsible decision making	☐	☐	☐
Practicing mutual respect	☐	☐	☐				
Communicating love	☐	☐	☐	Taking time for fun	☐	☐	☐

I learned:

I plan to change my behavior by:

CHAPTER 8

The Family Meeting

Democratic family relationships develop most effectively when all members have an equal opportunity to join in the decision-making process. Successful family meetings require these conditions.

The family meeting is a regularly scheduled meeting of all family members. The topics are their beliefs, values, wishes, complaints, plans, questions, and suggestions. It is an opportunity for all to be heard on issues arising in the family.

The family meeting is an appropriate time to plan family fun and to share good experiences and positive feelings toward each other. Regular meetings can promote family harmony by providing time for establishing rules, making decisions, recognizing the good things happening in the family, and pointing out strengths of individual members.

Some parents object to the idea of regular meetings. "We don't need them," they say. "Our family already holds a continual family meeting. We discuss things like this all the time."

Nevertheless, we urge that you set aside a routine time for family meetings, to promote a definite commitment on each person's part to share in family concerns. The meeting time should be convenient for everyone.

If some members decide not to attend, they will have to accept the logical consequences of not attending: For example, the rest of the family might make decisions which will affect them.

In summary, the family meeting provides opportunities for:

- Being heard.
- Expressing positive feelings about one another and giving encouragement.
- Distributing chores fairly among members.
- Expressing concerns, feelings, and complaints.
- Settling conflicts and dealing with recurring issues.
- Planning family recreation.

Guidelines for Family Meetings

1. Meet at a regularly scheduled time, so that family members can make their plans accordingly and can count on a time to discuss the issues important to them.

2. Share the responsibilities of the meeting itself by rotating who chairs the meeting. A parent can take the chair first, to model procedures. Then the family can plan a way to rotate the responsibility among children and parents.

The original chairperson should be a family member who believes in equal rights and democratic relationships. The chairperson starts and closes the meeting in line with times agreed upon. He or she makes sure that *all* points of view *are heard* and tries to keep members *focused* on the issue under discussion.

The method of rotation should, as stated earlier, be a group decision. Generally, a child

of school age can serve as chairperson with adult guidance. Adult intervention should be minimal — reminding the child of procedures if necessary, but allowing the child to lead the group.

3. Keep minutes of family meetings so that you have a record of issues, plans, and decisions. Some families find it helpful to post the minutes of each meeting so that family members can check the agreements made. The role of secretary should also be rotated. Children too young to write minutes might participate by being in charge of a tape recorder.

4. Together, plan the amount of time you will reserve for family meetings. They should not run over one hour with older children, and not over 20 to 30 minutes with young ones. Stay with your plans. Focus on the business at hand.

5. All family members must have opportunity to make suggestions about an issue under discussion. Parents, as well as children, join in making suggestions. If the children come up with appropriate ideas, parents should generally refrain from adding more.

Especially in the early stages of family meetings, it is important to withhold your suggestions until the children have finished giving theirs. If you "jump in" with suggestions right away, the children may feel you're trying to force your ideas on them. After the democratic atmosphere has been established, interactions back and forth can become more vigorous.

6. Guard against letting the meetings become gripe sessions. If griping becomes chronic, establish a rule that complaints will be heard only if the complainer is willing to seek a solution. (This can be done by asking the person raising

the problem whether she or he wants to solve it or only to complain about it.) The leader's function is to be sensitive to the complainer's feelings about the problem, send I-messages when appropriate, and keep the focus on "What can we do about it? How can we solve the problem?"

7. In deciding who will do the household chores, parents and children *together* make a list of necessary chores and then decide how to distribute them. Parents can initiate a spirit of cooperation by volunteering for the less desirable jobs themselves. (Of course, parents should not continue to volunteer only for the "worst" chores.) To avoid misunderstandings, the family needs to decide chore deadlines and what the consequences will be if deadlines are missed.

8. Any agreements made in the family meeting are to be in effect until the next meeting (in most cases, one week). Sometimes children will not keep their agreements. When this happens, parents can use logical consequences. Of course parents, too, are to honor agreements.

9. Any complaint about decisions from a meeting should be deferred until the next session. When a complaint about a decision is made during the week, "Bring it up at the family meeting" should be a consistent reply. If that statement is honored at the next meeting, family members thus learn that they have a reliable forum.

10. *All* family members must have opportunity to bring up matters important to them. If the meetings are dominated by issues only the parents want to discuss, the children may lose interest or not feel involved. The leader can encourage the children's involvement by asking, "Who has something she or he wants to discuss?"

Some families establish an agenda book which members sign if they wish to bring something up at the next meeting. After the agreements of the last meeting are reviewed, the chairperson refers to the first name on the list and begins the meeting with that person's topic. Members who do not get a chance to discuss their interests can be first at the next meeting. Members who want to bring up something, but did not sign up, may introduce their topics after those who did sign up are finished, if time permits.

11. Make sure your meetings are more than job-distribution and problem-solving sessions.

If they are limited to this, everyone's interest will fade. Be sure to provide time for recognizing the good things happening in the family. Family meetings are for encouragement and for planning family fun, as well as for problem solving.

Some families spend some recreation time together after each meeting. They feel this ends the meeting on a positive note.

Leadership Skills

Effective leadership keeps the meetings moving toward mutually agreeable solutions. It is based on respect for everyone's opinion.

The following guidelines will contribute to effective family meetings:

1. Use reflective listening to help family members feel understood.

2. Use I-messages to express your feelings and to model honest communication for other family members.

3. Pinpoint the real issues; do not be distracted by side issues. If the real issue is a matter of power, control, or personal privilege, point it out in a friendly manner; e.g., "It seems we are all interested in getting our own way. How can we deal with this?" Stay with the real issues.

4. Use brainstorming to identify possible solutions to problems brought up for discussion. Ask members to think of all the alternatives they can. Delay decisions until all ideas have been given. When it appears that all the possibilities have been identified, explore the implications of each one. Evaluate each suggestion. (For example: "How does everyone feel about drawing names to decide who does the chores?") Continue the evaluation procedure until the family finds a mutually acceptable solution.

Brainstorming allows each person to participate and provides an opportunity for members with opposing ideas to find another idea which appeals to all.

(NOTE: If done with mutual respect, this procedure encourages willingness to participate in generating solutions. If a member's suggestion is rejected as soon as it is said, the person will probably stop giving ideas. If evaluation is postponed until all suggestions have been given, a member's idea may be seen as one of many that are not accepted by the family. Thus, the rejection is seen as impersonal and is "softened.")

5. Work for consensus. Voting creates a competitive atmosphere in family meetings. The losers may resist implementing the decisions of the majority. Therefore, it is best to table any issue on which consensus is not reached. "It looks as if we're not ready yet to agree on a solution. Let's think of some other ideas this week and talk about them at our next meeting."

Occasionally an issue will need immediate attention. If consensus cannot be quickly reached, the parent can tell the family that he or she will have to make the decision. "It appears that we're not ready to make a decision on this yet. Something must be done about it right away, though, so I will make the decision and we can have another opportunity to discuss it at our next meeting."

Be cautious with this procedure. Closely evaluate whether an issue actually needs such immediate attention. Also be aware that if premature decisions are made — if the goal is not simply to do what the situation requires — you are inviting resentment and rebellion.

6. Summarize and obtain a commitment. At appropriate times during the meeting, clarify and summarize what has been discussed and decided. Then obtain a commitment. "So far, we have discussed_____and we have decided_____. Is everyone willing to follow this procedure until the next meeting?"

A final summary settles the decisions and commitments made during the meeting. "Today we decided_____. Is that the way everyone understands it?"

7. At the opening of each meeting, under old business, always ask the family to evaluate decisions made at the previous meeting. "How does everyone feel about the decision made about _____?" The family can then decide whether to keep the agreement or change it. Complete this reevaluation before proceeding to new topics.

When to Begin Family Meetings

You can start family meetings as soon as you and your spouse have a clear understanding of what the meetings should achieve and are ready to function as equals with each other and with your children. Parents who play the role of benevolent autocrat or passive resister will hinder progress. There must be a conscious decision to work together.

The children must also be ready to join discussions. If you initiate meetings before most of your children are ready, your chances for success are slim.

How do you determine when your children are ready? Although there is no way to be certain, a rule of thumb is to wait until you have worked through enough problems with your children and

"feel" the children are ready to cooperate; then assess how your children will respond to the idea. The idea of having regular family meetings might be discussed with the children individually or as a group. It is essential that the children be involved in deciding whether or not to have meetings. The decision should not be legislated by the parents. When the values of family meetings are explained, children are generally enthusiastic.

It is not necessary to wait until *all* family members are ready. If most are, it is appropriate to get started. Those who do not attend the early meetings might decide to join in later, after they find that decisions made in the meetings may affect them.

Establishing Meetings When Only One Parent Is Interested

If you have been working through STEP without your spouse, you may be wondering whether one parent can initiate family meetings. We find that one parent *can* conduct meetings if she or he briefly informs the family about the purpose of meeting and invites all who would like to participate. If your spouse refuses to participate, you and the children can still make many decisions which involve your relationship with them. When your spouse sees the benefits of the meetings, he or she may decide to participate.

Single parents can also gain more cooperation from their children by establishing family meetings. In the single-parent home, family meetings are restricted to matters outside the children's relationship with the absent parent. (If the children are concerned about the latter, those discussions should be held at other times when the parent can use reflective listening and exploring alternatives specifically to help them decide how to relate more effectively with the absent parent.) Family meetings are for the purpose of making decisions about issues that involve those living together.

Introducing Family Meetings to Young Children

You may be wondering at what age young children can be included in family meetings. We feel that as soon as children can communicate, they are ready for this experience. Keep the introductory meetings very brief and simple. Usually, participation in one issue per meeting is all one can expect of young children.

As you continue to meet and the children mature, you can move to longer, more formal meetings.

Initiating Family Meetings

There are many ways to start. Sometimes a formal procedure is well received by the children. From it, they can sense the importance of the undertaking. At the first (exploratory) meeting, the parents explain the purposes and procedures of family meetings and ask the children if they would be interested. If the children say yes, the format for succeeding meetings is as follows:

1. Read and discuss the minutes of the previous meeting.

2. Discuss old business, evaluating previous decisions and discussing unresolved issues.

3. Discuss new business, including plans for family fun.

4. Summarize the meeting, reviewing decisions and commitments.

If your children resist meetings that are formal or which emphasize chores, you may choose a more casual approach. For example, you might begin by planning a recreation activity in an informal session after dinner. You might say, "How about our doing something together this Sunday; perhaps some sort of outing? Does anyone have ideas about where we could go?"

After everyone agrees on the itinerary, the family can decide the time for the outing, who will do what in preparation, and so on.

When the day of the outing comes, expect the children to carry out the responsibilities they chose. If someone forgets, do not single him or her out, and do not rescue the situation. Let everyone experience the consequences.

Your goal is to reinforce teamwork and interdependence, not to play detective or overseer.

As family members learn to cooperate, you can informally begin to introduce problems and the necessity of household chores at another meeting. As the group becomes accustomed to working through problems and planning family fun, you can bring up the idea of establishing formal meetings so that all the family business can be transacted in one session each week.

Common Mistakes in Family Meetings

1. Waiting until every member of the family agrees to attend (instead of beginning with those who are willing).

2. Starting late.

3. Meeting for too long a time.

4. Domination by one or more persons (including parents).

5. Overemphasizing or focusing on complaints and criticisms.

6. Not putting agreements into action.

The family meeting can be a link that strengthens family ties. Although it is not a cure-all for family ills, its potential is considerable. It is an important element in the development of democratic family relations.

QUESTIONS

1. What is the authors' definition of a family meeting? Why do they believe family meetings are important?

2. Why do the authors suggest regularly scheduled family meetings rather than meetings only for emergencies?

3. What kinds of things can be discussed in the family meetings?

4. What are the suggested guidelines of the family meeting? Why is each guideline important? For example, why is it important to rotate the chairperson and secretary?

5. What leadership skills are necessary for effective family meetings?

6. When should family meetings be initiated?

7. How do you establish meetings if your spouse is not interested?

8. What are the guidelines for single-parent family meetings?

9. How can family meetings be established with young children?

10. What are some suggested ways of initiating family meetings?

11. What are some common mistakes made in family meetings?

PROBLEM SITUATION

Mr. and Mrs. Ford have three children: Bill, ten; Melissa, nine; and Sally, six. They decide to introduce family meetings by planning a family outing.

Bill and Sally decide they want to go to a movie, but Melissa wants to go to a baseball game. Mother would prefer the movie. Father would like to go to the game, but is willing to go to the movie if the rest of the family would rather go there. Melissa refuses to go along with the rest of the group.

1. What might be keeping this family from more productive problem solving?

2. What guidelines for family meetings are recommended to make progress?

3. What options are available to the Ford family for resolving this deadlock?

ACTIVITY FOR THE WEEK

Hold a family meeting this week.

CHART 8

Essentials of Family Meetings

The family meeting is a regularly scheduled meeting of all family members who want to attend.
The purpose is to make plans for family chores and family fun,
to express complaints and positive feelings, to resolve conflicts,
and to make other sorts of decisions.

Guidelines for Family Meetings	Pitfalls to Avoid
1. Meet at a regularly scheduled time.	1. Meeting only to handle crises; skipping meetings; changing meeting times.
2. Treat all members as equals. Let everyone be heard.	2. Dominating by members who believe they have more rights.
3. Use reflective listening and I-messages to encourage members to express their feelings and beliefs clearly.	3. Failing to listen to and encourage each other.
4. Pinpoint the real issues. Avoid being sidetracked by other issues.	4. Dealing with symptoms (such as bickering and quarreling) instead of the purposes of the behavior.
5. Encourage members by recognizing the good things happening in the family.	5. Focusing on complaints and criticisms.
6. Remember to plan for family fun and recreation.	6. Limiting the meetings to job distribution and discipline.
7. Agree upon the length of the meeting and hold to the limits established.	7. Ignoring established time limits.
8. Record plans and decisions made. Post the record as a reminder.	8. Failing to put agreements into action.

POINTS TO REMEMBER

The Family Meeting

1. The family meeting is a regularly scheduled gathering of all members of the family. Its purpose is to discuss ideas, values, and complaints and to plan family work and play.

2. The family meeting provides opportunities for:

    a. Being heard.

    b. Expressing positive feelings about one another and giving encouragement.

    c. Distributing chores fairly among members.

    d. Expressing concerns, feelings, and complaints.

    e. Settling conflicts and dealing with recurring issues.

    f. Planning family recreation.

3. Rotate chairperson and secretary.

4. Parents should model the communication skills of reflective listening, I-messages, and problem-solving so the children can learn more effective ways to communicate.

5. When progress is blocked, pinpoint the real issues (such as a member's desire for winning power, control, or special privilege). Do not be sidetracked by side issues such as a chore or specific event.

6. Take time to recognize the good things happening in the family. Encourage each other!

7. Plan the amount of time you will meet, and stay within those limits.

8. All members participate as equals.

9. The family meeting is not a "gripe" session, but a resource for solving problems.

10. Focus on what the group can do rather than on what any one member should do.

11. The goal of the family meeting is communication and agreement.

12. Follow through on agreements.

13. Try to see and understand each other's points of view.

14. At each meeting:

    a. Read minutes reporting topics and decisions covered at the previous meeting.

    b. Discuss unresolved issues and/or decisions which may need to be changed.

    c. Bring up new business and plan family fun.

    d. Summarize points considered and clarify commitments.

My Plan for Improving Relationships

(An opportunity to assess progress each week)

My specific concern:

My usual response:

- [ ] talking, lecturing
- [ ] noticing, nagging
- [ ] becoming angry

- [ ] punishing, removing privileges, shaming
- [ ] threatening, warning
- [ ] other_____

My progress this week:

	I am doing this more	I am doing this less	I am remaining about the same		I am doing this more	I am doing this less	I am remaining about the same
Listening	[ ]	[ ]	[ ]	Withdrawing from conflict	[ ]	[ ]	[ ]
Acting firmly and kindly	[ ]	[ ]	[ ]	Using consequences	[ ]	[ ]	[ ]
Becoming consistent	[ ]	[ ]	[ ]	Stimulating self-reliance	[ ]	[ ]	[ ]
Encouraging	[ ]	[ ]	[ ]	Stimulating responsible decision making	[ ]	[ ]	[ ]
Practicing mutual respect	[ ]	[ ]	[ ]				
Communicating love	[ ]	[ ]	[ ]	Taking time for fun	[ ]	[ ]	[ ]

I learned:

I plan to change my behavior by:

CHAPTER 9

Developing Confidence and Using Your Potential

In STEP you have studied human behavior and developed procedures for improving your relationships with your children. We hope you feel that this training has helped you grow as a person and as a parent.

Even though you have devoted time and effort to improvement, your road ahead won't always be smooth. At times you may feel discouraged. "After all I put into this," you may say, "I deserve fewer problems with my children!"

We tend to think of growth and learning as a diagonal line — "onward and upward." Actually, however, new learning progresses more like the incoming tide — we move forward, retreat, move forward more, fall back. The falling back is discouraging if we don't realize that when we move forward we are a little ahead of where we were previously.

Discouragement can be avoided by setting realistic goals. Do not expect the beds to be made perfectly, the dishes to be spotless, or things to run smoothly all the time. At times your children may choose new misbehaviors to test you. You are dealing with human beings, and they will make mistakes. You must have the courage to be imperfect and to allow them to be imperfect too. If you can accept your own imperfect ways of trying to change and, with a sense of humor, understand your own errors, you will be free to accept your children's.

Optimism is based on a sense of personal worth and identity which goes beyond one's role as a parent. You need to take an inventory of your assets and establish who you are. You are probably effective at your work, have friends, and get along reasonably well with members of the opposite sex. What are some other things you value about yourself? Your patience, sense of humor, capacity for friendship, loyalty, kindness, concern for others? You can probably add to this list.

When you finish STEP, you may still be struggling with one of its principles — with the idea of equality for all members of the family. Many parents have a hard time accepting this idea. They are reluctant to give up their position as rulers of their own households. In effect, however, in many households authoritarian parents have already "given up the throne," with the result that the real rulers are the children.

The equality that STEP urges is, in a sense, a statement of the rights of both parents and children. STEP is designed to free you from the yoke of servitude to your children and to restore your rights in the family. In this process your children will experience their responsibilities and their rights.

Another principle this course has stressed is that to improve yourself as a parent, you must

be willing to change. You must also believe that procedures *are available* to help you become a more effective parent.

In our attempt to influence others to change their behavior, we must accept the fact that the only tool to which we have direct access is our *own* behavior. Once we accept that our purpose is not to change other people, we are ready to take responsibility for ourselves and to accept others as they are. Acceptance of personal responsibility is a basic principle for personal growth (maturity) and for improving all human relationships.

By changing our own behavior we can influence our children to change. Our changed behavior is no longer reinforcing our children's mistaken goals. If they cannot achieve their goals of attention, power, revenge, or display of inadequacy, they will give them up and become more cooperative.

Remember the influence of both positive and negative expectations. If you believe your children will disappoint you or not perform, they will probably "live down to" your expectations. Expect that they will cooperate, and accept any good effort, and they will be more likely to try.

Accepting their efforts encourages them, improves your relationship, and builds their feelings of worth as well as your own. When you no longer feel you have to criticize and point out mistakes, you will be free to love and value others. By valuing and encouraging your children, you will get in touch with your own strengths too.

Expect to hear criticism of your new methods. When it happens, you may feel defensive and want to tell the critic the "right" way to raise children; or, you may be tempted to give in at the expense of your children.

Defensive reactions indicate that one's feelings of personal worth are at stake. When one's personal worth is threatened, errors in judgment follow.

If other adults do criticize your new methods, keep in mind that they may be expressing their own insecurities. (If they really felt secure, why would they need to criticize you?) When you receive criticism, call on your new communication skills. Through reflective listening, indicate to your critic that you understand his or her feelings. Through I-messages, let the person know how *you* feel. If appropriate, seek agreement. While you remain friendly with your critic, maintain your firmness about what you intend to do.

You must come to understand that your emotions have a purpose behind them, too. Have

you ever been in a heated argument, then suddenly answered the telephone or the door in a calm, pleasant manner? All of us can do it. This shows that we really are in charge of our own emotions. We feel as we believe. As we change our convictions and behavior, we can change our feelings.

When things don't go your way, you may believe it's horrible that you're being inconvenienced. It may be inconvenient, but it isn't horrible!

Understand, too, that your children are not the symbol of your success in life. If they do not behave "properly" or "succeed," you have not suffered a catastrophe. Your personal-asset inventory, not your children, can reassure you of your personal worth.

When things do not go well with your children, you may feel guilty about "failing them" or about your own lack of success. We believe that expression of guilt is a cover-up—the expression of good intentions that we do not really have. Most of us say we feel bad about not paying more attention to our parents or relatives or about not stopping some bad habit. By expressing our guilt, we try to convince others and *ourselves* that we really are thoughtful people even though we don't translate our intentions into actions. For some, the expression of guilt removes the necessity of acting. Obviously, however, feeling guilty can't change things. Action can!

Another hindrance to progress may be your own self-defeating patterns. The following are some faulty assumptions which interfere with personal growth and influence poor relationships:

"I feel that I want to be loved or approved of by everyone in my community."

"I must be competent in all aspects of child-training before I can consider myself personally worthwhile."

"It's a catastrophe when things don't turn out the way I would like."

"There really isn't much we can do about our problems. When it comes right down to it, we are really victims of circumstances."

"Disobedience from my son is a personal challenge to my authority as a parent."

"Children's background — their genes and their environment — determine their present behavior. There's very little we can do to bring about change."

"I, as the parent of my children, am responsible for my children's misbehavior. Since my children are only a product of what has happened between them and me, they wouldn't misbehave if I were a more effective person. I have only myself to blame."

To remain optimistic, it's important to accept our concerns with our children as challenges which can be overcome.

If we relate to our children with as much respect as we show our good friends, mutual respect will get us through difficult times.

A parent who has a strong sense of identity as a person of value, does not find it necessary to live through her or his children. Such a parent is free to face the challenges of life courageously.

QUESTIONS

1. What is meant by "the rights of both parents and children"?

2. What are the difficulties of giving up your position of power in the family? What are the benefits of giving up this power?

3. The authors believe that the parent, not the child, must be the first to change. What are the implications of this for the challenges parents face with their children?

4. How can unrealistically high standards interfere with effective parent-child relationships?

5. What do the authors suggest we do to avoid becoming discouraged in our relationships with children? What do they mean by setting realistic goals?

6. Why is it important to recognize our strengths which have nothing to do with being a parent? How do you feel about no longer seeing your children as symbols of your success or failure as a person?

7. What are some things we need to consider when others are critical of our child-training methods?

8. What happens when we feel guilty? How can we avoid inappropriate guilt feelings?

9. The authors mention faulty assumptions which interfere with our personal growth and bring about poor relationships with other people. Do you hold any of these beliefs? Which ones?

10. How can we begin to change these beliefs?

PROBLEM SITUATION

Mrs. Grant has been actively involved in learning how to become a more effective parent. Her children, Gloria, 12, Cheryl, 9, and Ron, 7, have become very helpful around the house. Without complaint they cut the lawn, weed the garden, and help with other household chores.

At a neighborhood open house for new parents on the block, the other parents began a discussion about the uncontrollable, uncooperative behavior of their children. Mr. Anderson said, "It's only a stage; you have to expect it. Our pediatrician says they'll grow out of it."

Mrs. Grant suggested that child-rearing procedures can be changed to correct certain types of misbehavior. Mr. Anderson replied, "I know your children are very helpful, but I want my children to enjoy childhood while they can, and not be forced to take on adult chores. I think you expect too much of them."

Mrs. Grant now feels she is in a dilemma: Has she really required too much of her children? But, why should she be expected to do all the chores herself?

1. What are some faulty assumptions expressed at the open house?

2. What faulty assumptions or beliefs may keep Mrs. Grant from continuing her program and the new relationship with her children?

3. Which of the faulty assumptions might hinder your own effectiveness?

CHART 9

Democratic and Positive Parenting

This chart points out (1) typical challenges of child rearing, (2) self-defeating
beliefs which may influence a parent to respond ineffectively and autocratically,
and (3) effective, democratic actions that can be used instead.

Challenge	Self-Defeating Belief	Ineffective, Autocratic Responses	Effective, Democratic Actions
Child talking back; sassing.	I must be respected and feared.	Demand an apology. Attack child verbally.	Ignore provocation or reflectively listen. If child continues verbal attack, send I-message and use logical consequence (withdrawal from unfriendly conversation).
Child not responding to request to leave on trip.	I must have an instant response.	Order, command, punish.	Send I-message or arrange so child experiences logical consequence (not going).
Child late in leaving for school.	My child can't walk in tardy. What would they think of me?	Nag, force, rush about.	Permit logical consequence (disapproval at school).
Children fighting and arguing.	I must settle disagreements. I am the judge.	Interfere, investigate.	Indicate confidence in child's ability to resolve own problem by withdrawing from the battle.
Child leaving belongings in living room.	It's easier to do it myself.	Nag, pick up after child.	Send I-message or use logical consequence (belongings are missed when wanted later).

Indicate a possible self-defeating belief and contrast ineffective/autocratic procedures with effective/democratic procedures for each of the following:

1. Child resisting bedtime. 2. Child not following through with chore agreed upon. 3. Child's hair too long.

Alternatives to Self-Defeating Beliefs

A number of the beliefs we commonly accept from our parents, society, and the media keep us from functioning effectively. They are often associated with discouragement, depression, anxiety, and the desire to control other people.

Here are some of the self-defeating beliefs, along with constructive alternatives:

1. (Self-defeating belief) It is necessary to be approved of by everyone in the community.

(Alternative) I will do that which makes me more liberated and self-confident and makes my children more responsible.

2. (Self-defeating belief) I must be thoroughly competent in all aspects of child training if I am to be considered personally worthwhile.

(Alternative) I do not get my feelings of worth from my children's behavior. I am more interested in improving my relationships than I am in perfection.

3. (Self-defeating belief) It is catastrophic and totally unacceptable when things do not turn out the way I think they should.

(Alternative) It is annoying and unfortunate when things don't turn out the way I'd like. I'll try to change the things I control and accept the things I have no control over.

4. (Self-defeating belief) Disobedience is a personal challenge to my status as a parent.

(Alternative) It is annoying not to be obeyed. I will try to find ways to improve the relationship so that my child will want to cooperate.

5. (Self-defeating belief) The child's background determines his or her present behavior; there is little I can do to change that fact.

(Alternative) The child's behavior has a purpose, and so I can influence it best by understanding the purpose and changing my reactions.

6. (Self-defeating belief) I can succeed with my children only if my spouse uses the same approach.

(Alternative) How my spouse behaves is his or her problem. I will be reponsible for my own behavior.

115

My Plan for Improving Relationships

(An opportunity to assess progress each week)

My specific concern:

My usual response:

☐ talking, lecturing   ☐ punishing, removing privileges, shaming

☐ noticing, nagging   ☐ threatening, warning

☐ becoming angry   ☐ other_____

My progress this week:

	I am doing this more	I am doing this less	I am remaining about the same		I am doing this more	I am doing this less	I am remaining about the same
Listening	☐	☐	☐	Withdrawing from conflict	☐	☐	☐
Acting firmly and kindly	☐	☐	☐	Using consequences	☐	☐	☐
Becoming consistent	☐	☐	☐	Stimulating self-reliance	☐	☐	☐
Encouraging	☐	☐	☐	Stimulating responsible decision making	☐	☐	☐
Practicing mutual respect	☐	☐	☐				
Communicating love	☐	☐	☐	Taking time for fun	☐	☐	☐

I learned:

I plan to change my behavior by:

To Learn More about STEP

Congratulations on completing STEP! We hope that the democratic concepts and methods of child training described in the *Handbook* have proved to be effective for *your* family. Other parents who are STEP "graduates" have reported several benefits, including

- increased knowledge of parenting
- improved relationships in their families
- improved communication with their children
- less conflict with their children

STEP Groups

For many parents, joining a STEP *support group* has led directly to improved parenting skills. By discussing the principles of STEP with other parents and the group leader, they have received support and encouragement from new sources. In a recent study, *over 93 percent* of the participants in STEP groups said they would indeed recommend the course to other parents.

We have also found that STEP group leaders are just as enthusiastic as parents about their parenting groups and the complete STEP program. Here's what some of them have written:

> "The STEP program should be mandatory for all parents!! Those who have participated in the program have seen many positive changes take place in themselves as well as their children. They feel STEP gives them the tools they need to meet today's challenge of raising children."
>
> Mary T. Kerr
> Guidance Counselor
> Orange Park, Florida

> "I have been a counselor and parenting educator for 15 years. I have over 20,000 counseling sessions to my experience, plus group work in all phases of mental health. Of all the material, the STEP program has been the most effective. I can only express my gratitude for the materials."
>
> Michael Plezbert, M.S.
> Counselor-Instructor
> Springfield, Missouri

> "Through STEP, parents become more patient. They feel they are not alone and have group support to share their concerns. STEP gives them confidence in themselves and the courage to make changes in their lives."
>
> Moya Jack
> Public Health Nurse
> Vancouver, British Columbia

"STEP excites parents and seems to speak truth to their hearts. The format allows openness and honesty — to create personal support."

Richard Kingsley
School Consultant
Portland, Maine

"When I discovered STEP, it answered my needs for an effective parent education program. We feel we have helped change many parents and families — all positive. We are in a wonderful situation — we inspire parents."

Chris Landon
Preschool Director
Indianapolis, Indiana

"STEP provides a convenient, effective, reasonably priced kit. I have parents who take more than one (course) and bring friends and relatives."

Janet Hagen
Social Worker
Hartford, Wisconsin

"I have been involved for three years — I love the program. STEP has really been great at putting my beliefs into practice."

Karen Logan
YWCA
Riverside, California

STEP in Your Community

If you are interested in joining or leading a STEP group, there are many organizations in your community that might be able to give you information. Check to see whether STEP groups are being offered by local schools, community centers, health centers, churches and synagogues, adult education programs, counseling centers, civic groups, psychologists, or social workers.

A Spanish version of STEP is also available to serve Spanish-speaking parents in your community: *Padres Eficaces con Entrenamiento Sistemático* (PECES). For additional details about PECES or about STEP groups, write to the publisher:

STEP/PECES Coordinator
AGS
Publishers' Building
Circle Pines, MN 55014

In Canada, write to:
Psycan Ltd.
101 Amber Street
Markham, Ontario L3R 3B2

In Australia, write to:
Australian Council for Educational
Research Ltd.
P.O. Box 210
Hawthorn, Victoria 3122